DELIGHTING IN CHRIST

ROOTED, BUILT UP, & ESTABLISHED

A STUDY ON THE BOOK OF COLOSSIANS

STACY DAVIS & BRENDA HARRIS

EDITORIAL TEAM

PASTOR CHRIS SWANSEN
Theological Editor, Calvary
Chapel Chester Springs

PASTOR STEVEN DORR
Pastoral Support, Calvary Chapel
Chester Springs

CARINNA LAROCCO
Copy Editor

JOAN PURDY
Copy Editor

MELISSA BEREDA
Graphic Designer

LYNN JENSEN
Office Support

CHRIS GOOD
Photographer

DELIGHTING IN CHRIST
ROOTED, BUILT UP & ESTABLISHED
A Study on the Book of Colossians
Part of the Delighting in the Lord Bible Study Series

© Copyright 2020
Calvary Chapel Chester Springs
PO Box 595, Eagle, PA 19480

ISBN 979 855 434 4886

Cover Design: Melissa Bereda
Cover Photo: RomoloTavani

Printed in the United States of America

TABLE OF CONTENTS

Stacy Davis

Stacy has been teaching women God's Word for over 15 years. She has learned many Biblical truths through difficult trials. Beginning at the age of three with her mother's brain aneurism, to the death of her fourth son and through invasive breast cancer, Stacy's faith has been tried and tested many times over. Her life gives testimony to God's redeeming and transforming power. Stacy teaches the truths of God's Word with passion, desiring to share with all women how to go through everyday struggles victoriously in Jesus Christ. She lives in PA with her husband, Barclay. They have six children.

Brenda Harris

Brenda's background in education, along with her many years as a classroom teacher, was foundational for the plans God had for her to serve Him. In 2006, she transitioned away from instructing young people how to read literature and began teaching women how they can have a closer walk with the Lord through reading and studying their Bible. She is an enthusiastic teacher who loves a great visual to help demonstrate practical ways to apply God's Word to real life. Brenda lives in PA with her husband, Michael, and their two children.

As you therefore have received Christ Jesus the Lord, so walk in Him, rooted and built up in Him and established in the faith as you have been taught, abounding in it with thanksgiving.

Colossians 2:6-7

To get the most out of this study, you will want to ensure the time you are studying God's Word is not just an academic exercise, but is for your personal application and life transformation. The goal of studying God's Word is to know God; who He is, what He has done, and why this is important for you. Studying the Bible should increase your faith in God. As you read the Bible, God is interacting with you. Your study time becomes a life-giving, life-changing experience, not just head knowledge. However, God's Word can only be personal and life-changing when the Spirit of the Living God is in your heart (John 14:17). As soon as this spiritual transformation takes place in your heart, the Holy Spirit communicates with your spirit all the Truths found in God and made known through Jesus Christ.

In 1 Corinthians 2:10–11, Paul says, "But God has revealed them [the truths of God] to us through His Spirit. For the Spirit searches all things, yes, the deep things of God. For what man knows the things of a man except the spirit of the man which is in him? Even so no one knows the things of God except the Spirit of God."

There is a story in the book of John about a Jewish man named Nicodemus. He was a Pharisee and member of the Jewish ruling council. He was trained in the Scriptures under the prominent Rabbi Gamaliel. In spite of his knowledge of God through his religion and position, he knew something was missing in his heart and life. Nicodemus knew Jesus was different. He was a great teacher, but even more, he knew God was with Him. Jesus told him that he must be born again to see the kingdom of God; that he must be born of water and the Spirit to enter the kingdom of God (John 3:3,5–6). The only way to be born again is through Jesus.

Jesus would later tell his disciples in John 14:6, "I [Jesus] am the way, the truth, and the life. No one comes to the Father except through Me."

Jesus is the only way to be born of the spirit and have eternal life. This is how the study of God's Word becomes personal. It begins with a personal relationship through faith in Jesus Christ. If you've never accepted Jesus as your Lord and Savior, turn to the Delighting in My Salvation section of this study. This is your first step.

All of the Delighting in the Lord studies use a study model we developed called R.E.A.D. This model takes you from reading the verses, to experiencing and understanding the details of the verses, onto applying them to your life, and finishing with delighting in God. The DITL studies are all verse-by-verse in their approach, allowing Scripture to interpret Scripture as you study. Our hope in writing these studies is that you will learn to understand the Bible and the heart of God.

Each week of study takes you through the R.E.A.D. approach. The week begins with an introduction to the verses being studied. Since Paul wrote the book of Colossians, we used a snapshot of his life in each opening section. He also is a wonderful example of a person who encountered Jesus and was changed from the inside out. His life testifies to what it looks like to be rooted, built-up, and established in Jesus Christ (Colossians 2:6–7).

Prayer

Luke 24:45 tells us that "He [Jesus] opened their understanding, that they might comprehend the Scriptures." After Jesus rose from the dead, He appeared before His disciples on numerous occasions. He spoke these words to them shortly before ascending into heaven. Jesus helped them understand the Scriptures; all that had been written in the Law of Moses, the Prophets, and the Psalms to that point.

It is the same for us. Jesus will open our understanding to the Bible.

For this reason, we encourage you to start in prayer every time you approach God's Word. Ask God to open your mind to His understanding, to make His Word clear to you, and to reveal to you an understanding of who He is.

RECEIVING GOD'S WORD

I love it when a delivery person appears at my door with a package. I am always so excited to find out what's inside the package. But first I must receive the package before I can open it. The Bible is like a package that we get from God. Every time we open it, we get to receive all the truths about God filled within the pages. The Bible is God's Word given to each of us so we will know Him and His Son, Jesus. My responsibility is to know what the Bible says. To receive it, I must read it. Otherwise, it's as if I left the delivered package sitting on the doorstep. I must open the door and take the package in for myself. This is the receiving part of our approach. It is rather simple. With each week of study, start by reading the designated verses from beginning to end.

By reading all the Scriptures being studied that week, you'll begin to see the context of what is being said. During the Receiving part of the study, you are reading for the big picture overview.

EXPERIENCING GOD'S WORD

The Experiencing portion of the study is where you will interact with God through His Word. It is here that God's Word gets broken down into bite-sized pieces. You will pull the verses apart through inductive and deductive questions to gain understanding of what God is saying. The questions will lead you verse-by-verse through the text to observe details, to see connections, and to interpret what is being said within context so that you can draw conclusions. This section will help you answer the questions, "Who, what, where, when, and why." There might also be questions that take you to other places in the Bible so you can see God saying the same thing but maybe in a different way. Our hope is that you will see the Bible as one continuous story this way.

Each week, we have broken up the entirety of the verses to be studied in Experiencing God's Word into smaller sections called Experience 1, Experience 2, and so forth. You may choose to do all of these sections at one sitting or space them out throughout the week.

continued

A few things to keep in mind as you work through Experiencing God's Word:

1. Try to use God's Word alone to answer each question. Commentaries and Study Bible notes should only be used after you've attempted to answer the questions on your own.

2. It's okay to leave an answer blank. I know we all like to have the "right" answer. But if you don't know how to answer a question, bring that question to your small group discussion time. The other women may be able to help you, as will the teaching session.

ACTING ON GOD'S WORD

In this part of the study, you will be applying the verses you've studied to your life. As you study God's Word, God will show you more about Himself. In turn, He will challenge us in areas of life concerning ourselves. This often demands something from each of us regarding our thoughts, emotions, reactions, relationships, and much more. As we see Him more clearly, we will see ourselves more clearly too. Hebrews 4:12 says, "For the word of God is living and powerful, and sharper than any two-edged sword, piercing even to the division of soul and spirit, and of joints and marrow, and is a discerner of the thoughts and intents of the heart." Through the Holy Spirit, God's Word will speak to the deep places of your life.

In this section you'll answer personal questions relating to the themes and points in the Experiencing section of the study. Be prayerful as you do the Acting section and allow God to search your heart for any areas of sin that may need confessing.

DELIGHTING IN GOD'S WORD DEVOTIONAL

Our ministry's foundational verse is Psalm 27:4, "The one thing I ask of the Lord—the thing I seek most—is to live in the house of the Lord all the days of my life, delighting in the Lord's perfections and meditating in his temple." In this final section, you will end by praising God for who He is. There is a short devotional pertaining to a verse you studied that week, and each one carries a gardening theme. This theme goes along with Colossians 2:6–7 which tells us to be rooted, built up, and established in Christ, similar to the imagery we see in God's creation. Each week ends with a section for praising God, delighting in Him, and resting in who He is.

Teaching Videos

There is a teaching video that accompanies each week of the study. The teaching should be considered a capstone on your personal study time. It is meant to tie everything together and to give you some additional insights into the verses that were studied that week. The teaching videos can be viewed by going to www.delightinginthelord.com. A teaching video set can also be requested for groups outside of Calvary Chapel Chester Springs. Please contact Stacy Davis and Brenda Harris through the ministry website: www.delightinginthelord.com.

COMMITMENT AND PLANNING

Dedication and a time commitment will be needed to get the full benefit of this study. Plan on setting aside 1–2 hours a week to complete the whole week's study. You will find that your investment in God's Word will be seen in your spiritual growth. Plan on coming to study with your weekly lesson completed.

BIBLE TRANSLATIONS

The DITL studies use the New King James version (NKJV) of the Bible when writing the study questions. You may find it easier to use this same translation. We recommend using a literal Bible translation such as KJV, NASB or ESV for the study if you don't use the NKJV.

BIBLE COMMENTARIES AND RESOURCES

We recommend that you don't use any Bible commentaries or resources until after you have studied the weekly verses yourself, allowing the Holy Spirit to direct your understanding. It can be tempting to read the commentary in study Bibles and online. Give yourself time to understand what is being said in each verse before turning to resources. We promise you that God will give you light bulb moments in your study time as you dig into the verses yourself.

In the study you may notice references to Strong's Concordance. It may look something like this: "Firstborn" is protokos (Strongs G4416). When you see this, it means that we are giving you the original word used in either the Hebrew (Old Testament) or Greek (New Testament) so that you can better understand the word usage. This often helps give a deeper understanding of what is being said through the use of that word.

Here are some suggested resources to use after you've completed each week's questions:

- The Bible Knowledge Commentary by Walvoord and Zook   • Warren Wiersbe Commentaries
- ww.blueletterbible.com   • Hebrew and Greek Lexicon
- Vine's Complete Expository Dictionary of Old and New Testament Words

HOW TO USE THIS STUDY

The DITL studies can be used individually or with small/large groups. If using on your own, we suggest doing the study pages over the course of a week then following up with the teaching video. If you are doing the study with a small or large group, we recommend all ladies complete the study on their own throughout the week. When the ladies meet, break them into small groups for discussion. The discussion should have a leader appointed to guide the discussion time. Keep the discussion to the study questions and verses being studied. Following the small group discussion time, watch the teaching videos as a large group or have the ladies watch later on their own.

The first week of study is an introduction week. There is no homework, and the introduction video may be watched at the start of the study. There is a Teaching Notes page for all the video lessons. For week one, this page is found at the beginning of the study. For all other weeks, it is found at the end of the week.

God desires a personal relationship with you. Maybe you've never heard that before. He loves you so much that He sent His Son, Jesus, to die on the cross for you. In His love for you, God provided His Son, Jesus Christ, to be the perfect sacrifice for your sin. When Jesus was crucified on the cross nearly 2,000 years ago, God put the sins of the whole world onto His perfect Son, Jesus, so that through Him you'd have forgiveness and eternal life. Jesus paid the penalty for your sin and provided a way to God.

The first step in receiving the forgiveness Jesus offers is by acknowledging you have lived your life apart from Him. You have followed your own motives and desires. In God's eyes, this is sin. Sin carries eternal consequences and separation from God. Salvation begins with repentance. Everyone must recognize they are sinful human beings in need of a Savior. Jesus is the answer to our sin problem. If you have never prayed to Jesus to ask Him into your heart, it is a simple prayer of acknowledging your faith in Jesus and asking Him to forgive you of your sins.

THE CONVERSATION WITH GOD IS LIKE THIS...

"Dear God, I admit I am a sinner and have lived my life doing what I want. You are perfectly holy, and I am not. My sin grieves You and separates me from You. Please forgive me."

"For all have sinned and fall short of the glory of God." (Romans 3:23)

"I believe that You provided Jesus Christ as the answer for my sin through His death on the cross. He paid my sin debt in full. He is my perfect substitute. Because of Him, I am cleansed forever from my sin."

"For the wages of sin is death, but the gift of God is eternal life in Christ Jesus our Lord." (Romans 6:23)

"Lord, please come into my heart and life. From this day forward, I desire to know You more and want to begin a personal relationship with You as my Savior and Lord. Thank You for Your free gift of salvation and that I am no longer separated from You but am filled with You by the power of the Holy Spirit."

"If you confess with your mouth the Lord Jesus and believe in your heart that God has raised Him from the dead, you will be saved." (Romans 10:9)

"Thank You, God, for forgiving me. Please help me to grow to know You better and to live a life that pleases You from this day forward. Amen."

If you have prayed to accept Christ as your Savior, please tell someone today! Share this exciting news with a close Christian friend, your small group leader, or your pastor. They will be thrilled to encourage you in your faith and your decision to follow Jesus!

WEEK 1
INTRODUCTION TO COLOSSIANS

Teaching Title _____

_____

_____

_____

_____

_____

_____

_____

_____

_____

_____

_____

_____

_____

_____

_____

_____

_____

_____

_____

_____

Teaching Videos Available for free at www.delightinginthelord.com

AS YOU GET STARTED

Before you begin this study, write down anything you already know about the book of Colossians:

INTRODUCTION

The book of Colossians was written by the apostle Paul (formerly known as Saul) to the church in the city of Colosse. This city was located east of Ephesus and at one time was a very large and strategic city. However, it declined into a smaller merchant town located near the trade route to Rome. It was considered part of a tri-city area with the cities of Hierapolis and Laodicea. It is believed that Paul evangelized the people in this town during his three-year stay in Ephesus as Acts 19:10b explains, "so that all who dwelt in Asia [Minor] heard the word of the Lord Jesus, both Jews and Greeks." Paul never personally traveled to Colosse. However, it is widely believed that one of the men who was converted under Paul's teaching, Epaphras (Colossians 1:7), took the good news he heard of Jesus Christ to Colosse and began the church.

Teaching about Jesus Christ was desperately needed for this young church filled with new believers. They needed to be grounded in their faith and their understanding of who Jesus was as well as what a life lived in Jesus Christ looked like. The church at Colosse was also struggling. They were beginning to believe heresies coming into the church. These heresies were a mixture of Judaism, Ascetism, and Gnosticism. Paul wrote this letter to encourage them in their faith and to help them understand these truths:

- The preeminence of Christ. He is over all things including creation.
- A believer is complete in Christ. Nothing else is needed.
- Redemption and reconciliation come through Jesus Christ. There is no other way.
- Christ is in the believer. Christ is our hope of glory.
- Beware of false teaching and heresy. Jesus is the all-sufficient, preeminent Savior.
- The believer must turn from old ways. A believer must put on the likeness of Christ.

Although Paul's message was very relevant for the people who initially read it, it still remains applicable. Many heresies try to invade our congregations of believers today. Whether it is the prosperity gospel, replacement theology, denying the deity of Christ, or rejecting the infallibility of the Bible, each one stands against the truth of what the Bible teaches. Therefore, we must remain diligent to be on guard against such false teachings. This letter reminds us to put Christ in His rightful place; He is to be above everything else.

AUTHOR

The apostle Paul, formerly known as Saul, is the author and identifies himself three times in the letter. It is believed he was imprisoned in Roman at the time this letter was written to the church at Colosse. Colossians, Philemon, Ephesians, and Philippians are known as the prison epistles. Paul refutes the false teachings coming into the church and points the young believers back to Christ. These new believers in Christ likely never had an in-person encounter with Paul and only knew him through his letters (Colossians 2:1).

PURPOSE

Paul heard of how things were going at the church in Colosse through Epaphras (Colossians 1:7-8). Much of what he heard was favorable, although he learned of heresy coming into the church. Paul was writing to the church at Colosse to encourage them in their faith and to purge doctrinal heresies that were invading the church, specifically teachings from Gnosticism, legalistic Judaism, and Ascetism. Paul's answer was to point them to Jesus and to remind them of who He is and who they are because of Him. Paul reminds the believers that in Christ they are rooted, built up, and established in the faith (Colossians 2:7).

One of the key verses central to the whole book is Colossians 1:18, "And He is the head of the body, the church, who is the beginning, the firstborn from the dead, that in all things He may have the preeminence."

DATE WRITTEN

Approximately 60-62 A.D.

MAP OF ASIA MINOR

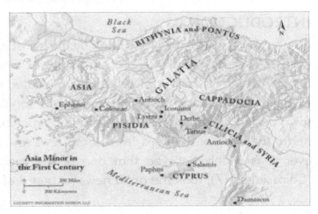

AS YOU GET STARTED

Summarize any information you gained after reading the introduction to Colossians.

In the space below, write a prayer to the Lord about what you hope to gain from Him as you study His Word.

WEEK 2
FAITH IN CHRIST

The Christian church was growing rapidly. Under the teaching of Peter and the other disciples, people were putting their faith in Jesus Christ and lives were changing. As word was spreading about Jesus from Jerusalem to the surrounding areas, opposition was also coming. A prestigious, religious Jew known as Saul (later called Paul) was hell-bent on halting the spread of the gospel by imprisoning the Jews who put their faith in Christ Jesus. With threats still fresh on his tongue against the faithful followers of Jesus, Saul set his sights on the believers in Damascus. Under the authority of the Jewish high priest, Saul headed towards Damascus to arrest believers and to bring them back to Jerusalem.

Unbeknownst to Saul, an encounter with the risen Lord awaited him that day. With Damascus visible in the distance, a light from heaven blinded his path causing him to drop to his knees. The voice of the Lord spoke to Saul, challenging his motivations and resistance to accept Jesus. The Lord spoke His purpose over Saul's life; a purpose defined by Jesus and for Jesus. The Lord told Saul that he wanted him to go to the Jews and the Gentiles to share Jesus with them. The Lord would use Saul to open the eyes of the people. He would bring them out of the darkness of this world and into the light of Christ; from the power of Satan to God. They would be forgiven of their sins and gain an eternal inheritance in heaven among all those who have put their faith in Christ Jesus (Acts 26:18). As the Lord's voice quieted and the blinding light was gone, so was Saul's vision. Left blind, the men who traveled with Saul led him to Damascus. It would be here that Saul would receive Jesus Christ as his Savior, be filled with the Holy Spirit, and be baptized. The moment we put our faith in Jesus Christ everything begins to change.

As word spread, people were shocked that a distinguished Pharisee like Saul, filled with murderous anger toward Spirit-filled believers in Jesus, could now be one of those very believers. He wasn't the same man, and people took notice. His faith was rooted in Christ and firmly established. He couldn't help but share the truth of Jesus with others. From persecutor to preacher, Paul became the most well-known missionary for sharing the good news of Jesus Christ wherever he went. From hostile Jewish leaders to Gentile audiences and Roman prison guards, Saul preached Jesus Christ. He planted churches, reached out to the sinner, and ministered to God's people. He would faithfully do this for over ten years before being arrested and sent to a Roman prison.

> THE MOMENT WE PUT OUR FAITH IN JESUS CHRIST EVERYTHING BEGINS TO CHANGE.

It is from prison that Paul would write his letter to the church in Colosse. A letter so important to the believer in Jesus Christ that God would include it in the Scriptures we hold in our hands today. A message that permeates time 2,000 years later. The same attacks that came against the believers in Colosse threaten believers today. The church in Colosse had heard of the gospel message Paul preached in the surrounding towns of Ephesus and Galatia. A man named Epaphras had been converted during that time and carried the gospel to Colosse. Over a short time, Epaphras witnessed the believers and the church come under attack, so he visited Paul in Rome to share his concerns and to ask him for help.

The young believers in Colosse were drifting in their understanding of the person and work of Jesus Christ. The church became the target of heretical attacks of trying to add and take away from the truth of the gospel. With zeal and fervency, Paul writes to the Colossian church and points them back to Christ. He speaks words of encouragement, thanksgiving, and love saying, "I've heard of your faith in Jesus, the way you are caring for each other, and loving well. I won't stop praying for you and your faith in Christ" (paraphrase Colossians 1:3–4).

Brenda and I (Stacy) are praying for you too. We are so thankful for you and your desire to know Jesus and to live lives pleasing to Him. God has a purpose for your life. Your life touches many people who need Jesus. He wants your life to be a reflection of His. May you be filled with His fullness and have spiritual understanding in the deep things of Christ. May you walk worthy of Him, fully pleasing Him alone. As your faith is placed in Christ and your life hidden in His, may He work mightily through you so that you bear fruit for Him in all you do, just like the Colossian church. May others say of you, as Paul said of the Colossians, "I've heard of your faith in Christ Jesus and your love for all the saints" (Colossians 1:4).

RECEIVING GOD'S WORD

Open in Prayer
Read Colossians 1:1–14

EXPERIENCING GOD'S WORD

EXPERIENCE 1: THE BASICS: WHO AND WHERE?

Colossians 1:1–2

WHO

1. Read Colossians 1:1. What do you learn about Paul and Timothy?

DEEPER EXPERIENCE

"He [Paul] was not one of the 12 Apostles (Acts 1:21–26) who were with Christ from the beginning of His earthly ministry. Nevertheless he did see the risen Christ (1 Cor. 9:1, 15:8–9), and he did possess special miraculous powers given to authenticate apostles (2 Cor. 12:12)." (Bible Knowledge Commentary, p. 669.)

2. The word "apostle" in Greek is Apostolos (Strongs 652). It means someone who is a delegate; an ambassador of the gospel; officially a commissioner of Christ (with miraculous powers): A messenger, he who is sent. Considering Paul probably never met the Colossians in person, why is this title used in verse 1 important for Paul to share with the Colossian believers?

3. Colossians 1:1 also mentions Timothy. Read Acts 16:1–3 and list anything further you learn about Timothy.

WHERE

4. Read Colossians 4:3. Where is Paul at the time of his writing?

5. From Colossians 1:2a, how does Paul describe the recipients of his letter?

6. According to Colossians 1:2b, where is grace and peace found?

    a. In your own words define grace and peace.

EXPERIENCE 2: IN CHRIST: BELIEVING AND ABIDING

Colossians 1:2–14

1. The word "in" is used multiple times throughout verses 2–14. Read the following verses and fill in the blanks below from the New King James Version of the Bible. It will make it easier.

    V. 2: brethren in _____

    V. 4: faith in _____

    V. 5: for you in _____

    V. 5: you heard before in the _____

    V. 6: the grace of God in _____

    V. 8: declared to us Your love in the _____

    V. 9: the knowledge of His will in _____ _____

    V. 10: being fruitful in _____ _____ _____

    V. 10: increasing in the _____ of _____

    V. 12: inheritance of the saints in the _____

    V. 13: conveyed us into the _____

    V. 14: in whom we have _____

2. There is a spiritual progression seen from these "in" statements that you just identified. Use your answers from the prior question to help you answer the following questions. You may need to reread the verses for context.

What does it mean to be "in Christ?" (v. 2 & 4)

How does this decision affect our future? (v. 5)

How is faith in Christ possible? (v. 5 & 6)

How does love operate with faith? (v. 8)

How does being in Christ affect decisions? (v. 9,10)

Describe how Christ changes the life of a sinner. (v.12–14)

If you don't know how to answer what it is to be "in Christ," please turn to the "Delighting in My Salvation" page in the beginning of the study. May today be the day that you put your faith in Jesus Christ.

EXPERIENCE 3: EVIDENCES OF FAITH

Colossians 1:3–8

1. Read Colossians 1:3–4. What was Paul hearing about the believers in Colosse? How did he support them from a long distance?

2. Verse 5 tells us that for those in Christ, our hope is laid up for us in heaven. Paul refers to the hope of heaven in Colossians 1:27 and 3:4 as well. Read those verses. The word "hope" means to have a confident expectation. Read 1 Peter 1:3–4. How does Peter describe our hope in heaven? How is this a confident expectation?

   a. In order to see the full picture of what is coming for the believer someday, how does Paul in 2 Corinthians 5:1–4 describe our hope of heaven?

3. Colossians 1:5–6 says that the "truth of the gospel" has been given to both those in Colosse as well as the "rest of the world." Read 1 Corinthians 15:3–4. What is the "truth of the gospel?" Who is central to the truth?

4. Colossians 1:6 says that the Colossian Christians were "bringing forth fruit." When did their lives begin to change?

   a. Read Galatians 5:22–23. What fruit should come from the life lived in Christ? Where does this fruit come from?

b. Based on Colossians 1:4–6, which fruits of the Spirit are being seen in the lives of the believers in Colosse?

5. In Colossians 1:7–8 we are introduced to a man named Epaphras. Read the verses below and note what you learn about him.

Colossians 1:7–8

Colossians 4:12–13

Philemon 1:23

6. Colossians 1:8 says that Paul heard about the love being shown among the believers in Colosse. Describe their love.

a. Read 1 Corinthians 13:1–13. What is the greatest evidence of a life lived in Christ? Why? Describe this Christ-like love in 1 Corinthians 13.

7. *The Bible Knowledge Commentary* says, "This trilogy of virtue—faith, love and hope is a favorite of Paul's (1 Cor. 13:13, 1 Thess. 1:3) and Peter's (1 Peter 1:3, 5, 22). Faith is the soul looking upward to God; love looks outward toward others; hope looks forward to the future." These virtues come from Jesus when a life is lived in Christ. They are possible because of the cross of Christ. Write faith, love, and hope on the cross illustration below. One word goes on the vertical representing our vertical relationship, one word goes on the horizontal representing our relationships with others, and one goes all around. Why are all these virtues tied together?

CROSS OF CHRIST JESUS

EXPLANATION:

EXPERIENCE 4: PRAYER FOR THE FAITHFUL

Colossians 1:9–14

1. In Colossians 1:9–14 Paul tells the believers in Colosse that he is praying for them. His prayer can be broken into four sections. We've listed these section headings for you. Read the verses and answer the following questions.

a. **Filled: (v.9)**

What does Paul pray the believers in Christ will be filled with? In your own words, describe each thing Paul references.

b. **Walk: (v. 10)**

How does Paul pray regarding the everyday walk of those in Christ? In your own words, describe what Paul identifies as being important in the walk of a believer.

c. **Endurance: (v. 11)**

Describe how Paul prays for the endurance of those in Christ. Where does power come from for a believer? Why is this important?

d. **Thankfulness: (v. 12–14)**

Paul is thankful to God for the believers in Colosse. Explain why he is thankful to God and what God has done for the believer.

ACTING ON GOD'S WORD

Paul gives us his prayer for the Colossian believers in Colossians 1:9–14. Remember that Paul never personally met these people but never stops praying for them. They were strangers to him, yet Christ united them all together in faith.

1. Have you found prayer to be a great unifier? If so, how did it break down barriers between people and draw you into closer fellowship?

2. Sometimes it is hard to know what to pray for another believer or even a stranger. Look at Colossians 1:3–14 and break down those verses into prayer points. An example is below:

   V. 3 Give thanks for that person

   V. 4 Pray for their faith and ask God to help them love others well through Christ

   V. 5

   V. 6

   V. 9

   V. 10

   V. 11

   V. 12

   V. 13

   V. 14

   a. How can you use this model in your prayer life? Who could you pray this over? Take a moment and pray for that person now.

3. Praying Scripture over an individual can be a powerful tool and way to pray too. I (Stacy) have often used Colossians 1:9–14 as a prayer for my husband. I've written Paul's prayer below. In the spaces provided, list the name of the person you would like to pray these verses over. Close by thanking God for this person, and then pray these verses back to the Lord.

For this reason, I, also, since the day I heard of it, do not cease to pray for _____ and to ask that _____ may be filled with the knowledge of God's will in all wisdom and spiritual understanding; that _____ may walk worthy of the Lord, fully pleasing Him, being fruitful in every good work and increasing in the knowledge of God; that _____ would be strengthened with all might, according to God's glorious power   for all patience and longsuffering with joy; I thank God, the Father for _____. He has qualified _____ to be a partaker of His inheritance of the saints in the light. He has delivered _____ from the power of darkness and conveyed _____ into the kingdom of the Son of His love, in whom we have redemption through His blood, the forgiveness of sins.

DELIGHTING IN GOD'S WORD DEVOTIONAL

"Stick...Put"
*"Since we heard of your faith in Christ Jesus
and of your love for all the saints"
Colossians 1:4*

My (Brenda's) sister-in-law, Marcy, shared a great gardening story with me that left a lasting impression upon me. One summer afternoon as she was walking in her neighborhood, she could not help but notice her neighbor's rose bushes. For many years she admired how they flourished and had such exquisite beauty. One day Marcy saw her neighbor outside and thought to herself, "I'm going to ask her about her rose bushes." Marcy approached her neighbor and complimented her on the beautiful flowers. She told her neighbor she had been admiring them regularly and inquired where she could purchase a similar rose bush for herself. Her neighbor, an older Italian woman who spoke broken English, motioned for Marcy to come closer. She ushered her toward the rose bush. She took a clipper and gave Marcy a branch from the rose bush. It had no roots or buds; it was simply a stick. Marcy looked quizzically at her and then back at the branch and said, "What do I do with this stick?" The kind woman pointed to the stick and then to the ground and said, "Stick...put." Looking puzzled, Marcy asked, "Just put this stick in the ground; that's it?" and the woman nodded. Marcy thanked her, took the stick, and followed her instructions. Sure enough, that stick eventually took root, and before long, Marcy had the most amazing rose bushes too.

In Colossians Paul describes a similar growth process happening with the church at Colosse. Whereas the people had once been dead in their sins, they now are demonstrating the effects of placing their faith in Jesus Christ. Paul is excited to hear about their faith and the love that resulted from their trust in Jesus. Their faith was like the stick Marcy received from her neighbor which had taken root in the soil of Jesus as their Savior. Their love was like the new growth which flowed from their faith in Christ. The church at Colosse had a true relationship with Christ. There was a fullness that was occurring inside them, and it was showing on the outside, much like the rose bushes. Paul is encouraged and compliments them for their growth as Christians.

If you have placed your faith in Christ, you too are growing. The "stick" of your faith is putting down deep roots, pushing forth leaves and beautiful flowers. Your growth may be smaller or slower than you would like but day by day it is developing. Each day is a new opportunity for your faith to strengthen, develop, and blossom. Before long, you may have the kind of faith that others ask about how to grow for themselves.

Praise God for the faith you have placed in Jesus Christ as your Savior.

Delight that you are loved by God.

Rest in the knowledge that growth is occurring in you.

Close in Prayer

Teaching Title _____

_____

_____

_____

_____

_____

_____

_____

_____

_____

_____

_____

_____

_____

_____

_____

_____

_____

_____

Teaching Videos Available for free at www.delightinginthelord.com

WEEK 3
IN CHRIST FIRST

When Saul opened his eyes, something that looked like scales had fallen away from his eyes and the face of Ananias came into clear focus. For three days Saul had been blinded. During that time, he sought the Lord through prayer and fasting. Ananias now stood in front of him with a tender, brotherly greeting in the Lord. Under God's instruction, Ananias placed his hands on Saul and prayed for his sight to be restored. He asked the Lord to fill Saul with the Holy Spirit. With prayers answered, Saul arose and was immediately baptized. He was transformed from the inside out by the living Christ. Despite Saul's long pedigree of Jewish birth, his education under the infamous Jewish Rabbi Gamaliel, and his many accomplishments, nothing held the same value as his encounter with Christ. From chief sinner to man of God, Saul was changed when Christ became Lord of his life.

Not long after his remarkable conversion experience, Saul, accompanied by Barnabus, was sent on his first missionary journey. Their travels would take them to faraway places to share the hope and truth of Jesus Christ with the Gentiles. Saul, also known as Paul, would become a mighty instrument in God's hands to build up the church over a period of nearly 20 years. During this time, Paul would author 13 books of the New Testament. He would be beaten, stoned, shipwrecked, and experience hunger and thirst as well as face all types of peril at the hands of his enemies. Despite all these trials, Paul wrote in the book of Romans that giving his body as a living sacrifice back to the Lord was his reasonable act of service.

Paul's heart was captured by Christ, and he came to understand Christ's power and authority over all things, including his own life. He reminds the church at Colosse of this very truth—Christ is preeminent over all things. Christ is first; everything else is second. God and Jesus have been One from before creation, and all of God's fullness is embodied in Jesus. These truths and others found in Colossians 1:15–23 dispel the lies which had invaded the church at Colosse and threatened the faith

> CHRIST IS PREEMINENT OVER ALL THINGS. CHRIST IS FIRST; EVERYTHING ELSE IS SECOND.

and steadfastness of the believers. Paul will remind the church that Christ was reigning before time and will still be reigning at the end of time. He is above all things and sustains all things in heaven and on earth. He is the firstborn from the dead; therefore, He is able to reconcile sinners back into a right standing before God. For these reasons, His rightful place is first over everything. This is the message Paul would write and preach to those he encountered. It was a life-changing message that continued to spread to the outermost places of the earth from then until today. May we each be captured like Paul with God's supremacy, power, and magnificence as we study these powerful truths, allowing them to sink deep into our hearts.

RECEIVING GOD'S WORD

Open in Prayer

Read Colossians 1:15–23

EXPERIENCING GOD'S WORD

EXPERIENCE 1: CHRIST'S SUPREMACY AND PREEMINENCE OVER CREATION

Colossians 1:15–18

1. Read Colossians 1:15. Jesus is presented as the image of God who is invisible. The word "image" in the Greek is *Eikon* (Strongs 1504). It means a copy or a prototype. It implies a likeness and a manifestation. It does not mean resemblance. Read John 1:18, 2 Corinthians 4:4, and Hebrews 1:3. How is Jesus both a likeness and manifestation of God?

   a. The second part of Colossians 1:15 says that Jesus is the firstborn over all creation. The word "firstborn" was borrowed from the Jewish upbringing. It refers to someone's place of honor. It does not mean that Jesus was the firstborn of creation because Jesus was not a created being. The word "firstborn" is *prototokos* (Strongs 4416). It speaks of rank and importance. Read Colossians 1:18, Hebrews 1:6 and Romans 8:29. What is Jesus' rank and importance in creation?

2. Read Colossians 1:16. Jesus created all things.

   a. What are the "all things" from this verse?

b. At the end of verse 16, two more important statements are made about Jesus and creation. Fill in the blanks below and explain what this is saying about Jesus. These blanks will be easier to fill in if you are using the New King James version of the Bible.

All things were created _____ Him.
Read John 1:3 for further help.

All things were created _____, _____, and _____ Him.
Read Romans 11:36 for further help.

3. What does it mean in Colossians 1:17 when it says Jesus is "before all things?" Read John 1:1–2 to give further understanding.

4. Verse 17 says that in Christ "all things consist." How does His power operate within both the spiritual and physical realm based on this verse?

5. In Colossians 1:18 we are told that "the body" is called the church. The body of Christ is made up of people who have put their faith in Christ. Read Ephesians 1:22–23. Describe the relationship between the body and Christ.

a. Look up the following verses about the body of Christ and note what you learn.

Romans 12:4–5

Ephesians 4:11–16

6. Paul repeated a phrase from Colossians 1:15 in Colossians 1:18. He says that Christ is the beginning, the firstborn from the dead. Read 1 Corinthians 15:20–23. What does "Christ is the firstborn from the dead" mean? What does this mean for those who are in Christ?

7. From Colossians 1:15–18, why is Jesus' rank, relationship with God, and his role in creation being established? Why is this important for a believer to understand?

EXPERIENCE 2: CHRIST'S SUPREMACY AND PREEMINENCE IN REDEMPTION

Colossians 1:19–23

1. Read Colossians 1:19. According to *The Bible Knowledge Commentary*, the word "fullness" means "complete" and the word "dwell" means "abide permanently." The Greeks had the idea that Jesus could not be human and divine at the same time. How does this verse refute that?

DEEPER EXPERIENCE

"God has willed that in Christ 'all fullness' should dwell. The word fullness is one of the key words of this letter, but also one of the most difficult to interpret. The word seems to have been in current use by the false teachers and was possibly employed by them for the totality of supernatural powers that they believed controlled people's lives. But to Paul, the totality of divine powers and attributes exists only in Christ; nothing of deity is lacking in Him" (Biblegateway.com; Expositor's Bible Commentary, Abridged Edition)

2. Read Colossians 1:20–22a. Describe how sinners are reconciled to God through Jesus Christ. Read Romans 5:8–11 for further understanding.

   a. How are unreconciled people (non-believers in Christ) described in verses 21–22a? How does hostility toward God affect our minds and actions?

DEEPER EXPERIENCE

"Reconciliation! Not once in the Bible is it ever said that God is reconciled to man. God has no need to be reconciled to us; we need to be reconciled to Him. The hostility is all on our part. God's hands are outstretched to us in love and always have been. We are the ones who have turned away. The hostility is always on man's side, not on God's side." (John Phillips, Exploring Colossians and Philemon, p. 70)

3. Read Colossians 1:22. What is the result of Christ's reconciling work in the life of the believer? How does Jesus present us before the Father once we put our faith in Him?

4. In the Old Testament holiness was ascribed to people, places, and sacrifices. Look up the verses below and explain how holiness is being attributed.

   a. People: Leviticus 20:7

   b. Places: Deuteronomy 23:14

   c. Sacrifices: Leviticus 22:21

   d. Read 2 Corinthians 5:21. Because of Christ's work on the cross, how does God see those who have been reconciled with Him through Christ?

   e. What is the main idea regarding holiness that Paul was conveying? Would you describe it as excellence of character or consecration (setting apart for dedication)? Explain your answer using the information you just learned.

5. Read Colossians 1:23. We should take note that this verse begins with the word "if." Paul speaks of a continuance of faith which gives the idea of permanence. For those who have been reconciled to God through Jesus Christ and have the righteousness of Christ, Paul uses three verbs to describe how the Colossian church should continue in the hope of their faith. List the three verbs.

a. How do these three verbs express a seriousness and permanence about pursuing Christ and trying to follow Him with all diligence?

b. Read Ephesians 3:17–19. Here Paul uses the words "rooted" and "grounded" instead of grounded and steadfast. What is the effect of being rooted and grounded in Christ according to the verses in Ephesians?

6. From Colossians 1:23, how did the Colossian church receive the gospel?

7. Describe the life-changing effect Paul says the gospel had on his life in verse 23.

8. We learned in Colossians 1:15–23 some very important things about Jesus. These truths about who Jesus is and what He has done are seen in these verses through the use of the words "He is," "by Him," "in Him," and "He has." For the sake of summary, reread these verses. Each time you see these words, write the truths about Jesus below.

ACTING ON GOD'S WORD

We have been examining the supremacy and preeminence of Christ in this lesson. This is sometimes a difficult concept to put into practice. Although we may want to give Christ a prominent place in our lives, even say we have put our faith in Him as our Savior, we may be unwilling to allow Him to have sovereign preeminence over all things. We say Christ is first; yet, we often live like He is second and we are first. Let's look at this as we apply the verses from this lesson to our lives personally.

1. Explain the difference between placing your faith in Jesus Christ as Savior, and placing your faith in Jesus Christ and then allowing Him to have preeminence as Lord.

2. In our lesson we learned about the "all things" Christ is preeminent over. Below is a list of specific areas of life. Place a star next to the ones you feel you have given Christ preeminence and authority over. Place a checkmark next to the ones that you do not feel Christ has all authority over.

_____Spouse/Marriage

_____Boyfriend/Dating

_____Finances

_____Children/Grandchildren

_____Work

_____Service to God

_____Gender/Sexuality

_____Emotions

_____Appetites

_____Health

_____Education

_____Other _____

a. Now look at your answers with a checkmark. Explain why Jesus doesn't have preeminence over this area. Often, we don't allow Jesus to have authority over an area of life because we are believing a lie about Him. Are there any lies you are believing that are inhibiting you from giving Him control?

b. In the topic(s) you checked above, is there any one specific thing that you think God is asking you to do? Write it down and ask Him for the faith to put Jesus first today. God would love to change all of our checkmarks to stars.

DELIGHTING IN GOD'S WORD DEVOTIONAL

"And He is before all things, and in Him all things consist. And He is the head of the body, the church, who is the beginning, the firstborn from the dead, that in all things He may have the preeminence."
Colossians 1:17–18

We lived in our home for more than ten years before we decided to properly tackle the acre of grass on our property. Up until then, the only care we had given to the grass was cutting it and an occasional fertilizer treatment. Having beautiful grass just wasn't a priority for us. We had growing children who rode their bikes through the grass and played countless sports in the yard. The yard was a playground area, yet it wasn't a blanket of soft, lush green grass. It was filled with weeds and bare spots. I remember having grass envy and wondering how people had such vibrant and beautiful grass growing in their yards.

One fall my husband decided that we would turn our attention to the lawn. He knew just using weed-killer and seeding the bare spots just wouldn't cut it; the yard needed an overhaul. Within days of making this a priority, I remember hearing a huge truck pull up to our house. I looked out the window, and I saw a bulldozer being unloaded from a flat bed. My husband wasn't joking around! After talking to a landscaper friend, he rented the biggest machine possible to scrape away the layer of weedy grass so he could get to the soil. This is the most important spot to focus on when growing grass. See, the secret to a healthy lawn lies in the soil.

We went to work. The top layer of grass was bulldozed away until all that was left was a yard filled with dirt. Then the real work began as the ground was tilled, and nutrient-rich soil was mixed in with the dirt along with some lime. Finally, the soil was ready for the seed. The next season our front yard was filled with beautiful, lush green grass free of weeds!

Colossians 1:17–18 tells us that Christ must have the preeminence over all things in our lives. Christ must be first. The soil is like Christ in our lives. He is the secret to the abundant life. When life looks weedy or lacking vibrancy, like our grass did, we may be tempted to tackle the problems with our own resourcefulness instead of going right to Christ. Instead of allowing Him to work through our troubles, we use worldly fertilizer or weed control. We may try to take control of life situations while the answer all along is found in the deep soil of our relationship with Jesus. Sometimes, we too need a bulldozer to show up in our lives and scrape away all that is in our hearts which is preventing Christ from having His rightful preeminence in all things. Our lives need to go back to the simplicity of rich, life-giving soil. That is the place where all things must begin.

Praise God for giving us Jesus and for making Him first in all things.

Delight in the richness of Jesus.

Rest in His preeminence in your life.

Close in Prayer

Teaching Title_____

_____

_____

_____

_____

_____

_____

_____

_____

_____

_____

_____

_____

_____

_____

_____

_____

_____

_____

_____

_____

_____

_____

_____

Teaching Videos Available for free at www.delightinginthelord.com

WEEK 4
ROOTED IN CHRIST

About 13 years have passed since Saul met Jesus on the Damascus Road and his life has changed. He had been faithfully serving the Lord and ministering to the Jews at Antioch in Syria at the time when the Jews were fleeing Jerusalem due to persecution. Sent out from the church at Antioch and under the direction of the Holy Spirit, Paul took Barnabas with him on his first missionary journey.

In Paphos they are confronted with a Jew named Bar-Jesus. He was a sorcerer who had influence with the deputy official in that country. People knew that Paul was preaching Jesus everywhere he went. As Paul and Barnabas came to town, the Roman proconsul, Sergius Paulus, called for Paul and Barnabas and asked them to share the word of God with him. However, Bar-Jesus stood in the way as he sought to turn Sergius Paulus away from putting his faith in Christ. Paul knew his scheme. He knew his motivation. Bar-Jesus wanted to pervert the gospel by preventing the scattering of the seed and hindering it from being established. Paul was quick to recognize this man's deceptive ways. Filled with the Holy Spirit, he looked intently at Bar-Jesus and said, "You are full of all deceit and all fraud, you son of the devil, you enemy of all righteousness, will you not cease perverting the straight ways of the Lord?" (Acts 13:10). Then the Lord blinded him. Being an eyewitness to the power of the Holy Spirit, Sergius Paulus put his trust in Jesus and allowed his life to take root in Jesus.

Very quickly Paul saw the power that wanted to come against the gospel of Christ. He saw the tactics being used; deceptive and persuasive words aimed at the person and the ministry of Jesus Christ. Words have power that can be used either for good or for evil. Paul would not let anything hinder the spread of the gospel. It was too precious. Christ was too powerful and life-altering. People needed to put their faith in

> PAUL WILL PLEAD EARNESTLY FOR GOD'S PEOPLE AND PREACH BOLDLY FOR THEIR FAITH TO TAKE ROOT AND TO BRING FORTH BEAUTIFUL FRUIT.

Him. They needed their walk to be rooted and established in Him. Colossians 1:24–2:7 tells us that it was this very deception that Paul was hearing about from Epaphras. Paul's soul was troubled upon learning what was happening among the believers in Colosse and in the neighboring town of Laodicea. His soul was in an all-out struggle for the lives of God's people. It was a struggle Paul brought to God in prayer. We need to do the same when we see the enemy come against the gospel of Jesus Christ and His people.

The enemy will stop at nothing to keep you out of God's kingdom or will try to make you ineffective once you are in God's kingdom. The verses we will be studying show us Paul's heart, once again, for all believers. He loves Christ and His people so much that he will suffer physically for the spread of the gospel. Paul will plead earnestly for God's people and preach boldly for their faith to take root and to bring forth beautiful fruit. As Christ is in you, let Him work through you, just as Paul did, so that you can combat the enemy and build up the people of God in Christ Jesus.

RECEIVING GOD'S WORD

Open in Prayer

Read Colossians 1:24–2:7

EXPERIENCING GOD'S WORD

EXPERIENCE 1: CHRIST IN ME: PAUL'S EXAMPLE

Colossians 1:24–29

1. Read Colossians 1:24. Describe Paul's current condition and why he is able to say it comes with an attitude of joy.

DEEPER EXPERIENCE

"Paul's words, **I fill up in my flesh what is still lacking in regard to Christ's afflictions,** did not mean that Christ's suffering was inadequate to save people. Paul believed that Christ's suffering on the cross alone paid for believers' salvation from sin: 'All have sinned...and are justified freely by His grace through the redemption that came by Christ Jesus. God presented him a sacrifice of atonement, through faith in his blood' (Romans 3:23–25)."
(Philippians, Colossians, Philemon, pg. 169)

2. After years of preaching to the Gentiles about Jesus, Paul is in Jerusalem to make an offering during the time of purification. The Jews from Asia see Paul in the temple and they are angry. Read Acts 21:27–30 and describe their accusation against Paul and what followed.

3. While Paul was being detained, the commander learned that Paul was a Roman citizen. This presented a problem because Roman law stated that no Roman citizen could be chained, scourged, or killed without a proper trial. The commander has Paul go before the Jewish Council so he can hear the accusations against him. After the commander puts Paul back in the barracks, some Jews formed a plot in an effort to kill Paul. The commander learns of this plot and preempts it by getting Paul quickly out of Jerusalem. He sends Paul to Felix, the Judean governor, before the Jews can accomplish their plan. After a few days, Felix listens to the accusations against Paul and allows Paul to speak. Read Paul's response to the accusations in Acts 24:14–16. How did he respond?

4. After being arrested, Paul shared the gospel with Felix. It seems that Felix didn't know what to do with Paul so he left him in prison in Caesarea for two years. During that time, Felix is succeeded by Festus. Eventually, Paul would ask that his case be appealed to Caesar. Sometime later Paul is brought to Rome in chains for his case to be heard. Read Acts 28:17–20 and 30–31. Describe Paul's situation.

5. Read the following verses about suffering in the life of the believer and note what you learn. Keep in mind that Paul wrote these words about suffering with the perspective of faith and experience.

   Romans 5:3–5

   Romans 8:17

   2 Corinthians 1:5–7

   Philippians 1:29

6. Like Paul, when we say "Yes" to God regarding ministry, we are fulfilling the word of God according to Colossians 1:25. Read Matthew 28:19–20. How does our service to God fulfill the word of God?

7. Read Colossians 1:26–27. The word "mystery" is used two times in these verses. In Greek the word is *musterion* (G3466). It means a truth that is revealed by divine revelation. Something that was once a secret is now revealed in the gospel. Answer the following questions from these verses.

   a. How long has the mystery been hidden? (v. 26)

   b. Who has it been revealed to now? (v.26–27)

   c. Read Romans 11:25. How do the Gentiles know of this mystery?

   d. What is the mystery? (v.27)

8. Read Acts 9:15 and 22:21. Now tie Paul's commission to Colossians 1:25–27. How is he fulfilling his commission from God?

9. Often ministries have a mission statement which defines their purposes and what they hope to accomplish. Read Colossians 1:28–29. Based on these verses, summarize the purpose for Paul's mission.

10. The word "perfect" means complete in work, growth, mental and moral character; someone who is lacking nothing and mature. In Colossians 1:28 Paul is speaking of the believer's daily walk in Christ. Look up the following verses about being perfect in Christ and note what you learn.

    Matthew 19:21

    2 Corinthians 3:18

    2 Corinthians 12:9

EXPERIENCE 2: CHRIST WORKING THROUGH ME
Colossians 2:1–7

In chapter 2 we will encounter one of the key reasons Paul wrote his letter to the Colossians. He was concerned about heresy and false religions which were beginning to infiltrate the church at Colosse. Below are definitions taken from Merriam-Webster's Dictionary.com. They describe the primary groups that Paul will come against. He will use the truth of who Jesus Christ is and what He accomplished on earth to refute their lies.

Gnosticism:
The thought and practice especially of various cults of late pre-Christian and early Christian centuries distinguished by the conviction that matter is evil, and that emancipation comes through gnosis (esoteric knowledge of spiritual truth held by the ancient Gnostics to be essential to salvation).

<u>**Jewish Legalism:**</u>
The strict, literal, or excessive conformity to The Law to attain spiritual perfection.

<u>**Asceticism:**</u>
The practice of strict self-denial as a measure of personal and especially spiritual discipline; the condition, practice, or mode of life of an ascetic; rigorous abstention from self-indulgence.

1. Read Colossians 2:1–4 and answer the following questions. Keep in mind that these verses are thought to be another prayer Paul prayed over the believers in Colosse and Laodicea.

    a. In verse 1 Paul expresses deep emotion toward the believers. From this verse we learn Paul had not seen any of these believers face-to-face. What is happening in Paul's heart regarding these churches?

    b. The word "conflict" (NKJV; Strong's 73) describes a struggle similar to one that takes place in an athletic contest. How is Paul using prayer as his weapon?

    c. How does Paul want the believers to be encouraged? (v.2)

    d. What is their confidence and why should this strengthen them? (v.2)

    e. What acknowledgement does Paul make in verse 3 about Christ?

f. Use verse 4 to describe what is happening in these churches. Why would this create a struggle in Paul?

2. Read Revelation 3:14–22. Christ is speaking about the church in Laodicea. What do you learn about this church and the warning that Christ gives them?

3. Read the descriptions above of the false teachings that were permeating the Colossian and Laodicean churches. How would Paul's reminders in Colossians 2:2b–3 help to refute these heresies?

4. Read Colossians 2:5a. Paul tells the church at Colosse that he is with them in spirit. What does that mean? How is that possible?

5. In Colossians 2:5b Paul recognizes some of the positive things he has heard about the church. What are they and why would this help them defeat the lies that were coming against their faith in Christ alone?

6. Read Colossians 2:6–7. Paul uses four words to describe the life of someone who has received Jesus Christ into their heart. The words are listed for you below with two verses. Describe each word. As you consider the action associated with each word, look up the verses to supplement your descriptions.

Walk [in Him]
Psalm 1:1; John 10:27

Rooted [in Him]
Psalm 1:3; John 15:5

Built up [in Him]
Ephesians 4:15–16; 1 Peter 2:5

Established [faith in Him]
1 Thessalonians 3:12–13; 1 Peter 5:10

ACTING ON GOD'S WORD

When you answered the last question (number 6) of Experience 2, you examined the concepts of walking, being rooted, built up, and established in Christ. We provided supplemental verses for you to examine in order to gain a broader picture of each action. Let's examine each of these actions and apply them to our lives.

WALKING IN HIM

1. Take a look at the descriptions below. Check off which of these descriptions you feel captures your walk with Christ right now.

    _____I am not walking with God

    _____I am walking behind God

    _____I am walking in step with God

    _____I am walking in front of God

    _____Other (Describe)

2. When a child first learns to walk, they often fall more than they walk. But as time goes by, the skill of walking becomes easier and easier, and before long, they aren't walking; they are running! Are there benefits to walking and falling? What happens if we run instead of walk with God?

ROOTED IN HIM

3. The phrase "rooted in Christ" gives the picture of a plant or tree with roots growing into the ground. If a tree is not securely grounded by its roots, what can happen to the tree?

4. The Christian life can be compared to the analogy of a tree. The tree is the person and its roots are representative of their grounding in Christ. Have you, like a tree, ever experienced a weak root system, being uprooted and transplanted, or even being knocked over in a storm? Describe what happened and how you became reestablished back into the soil once again to grow stronger, deeper roots.

BUILT UP IN HIM

5. Describe how your life is built up in Christ. Give an analogy for a life that is built up in Christ.

ESTABLISHED IN FAITH

6. When something is established, it can indicate something new has been completed. Sometimes a time frame, event, or circumstance will be the indicator to remember the milestone event. What marks the day you were established in Christ? Describe it.

    a. Once something is established, it needs to be maintained. How are you providing maintenance for your faith so that it remains steadfast?

"Easter Flowers"

"As you therefore have received Christ Jesus the Lord, so walk in Him, rooted and built up in Him and established in the faith as you have been taught, abounding in it with thanksgiving."
Colossians 2:6–7

Growing up in a family of farmers gave me (Brenda) a unique perspective of growing plants. I lived near my dad's side of the family, and my great uncle had a large greenhouse on his property. I remember spending quite a bit of time there, especially near Easter time.

It took approximately 8 months of preparation in order to be ready to sell the plants to the public by Easter weekend. It all began the previous fall when the bulbs were placed in pots, covered with sand, and stored in a cool, dark place for the winter months. As they wintered, the bulbs began to develop roots. These roots were essential to the life of the plant to come. No one saw the roots growing, but my family knew from years of experience they were developing silently while waiting for spring.

In order for the plants to be blooming by Easter weekend, they needed to be removed from the dark in just the right time frame. One by one each bulb was shaken from its sandy winter location and transferred to the big greenhouse where there was rich soil, bright sunlight, and protection from the cold night air. Before long, tall green foliage began to emerge, and with careful attention, the plants reached maturity. I can still remember walking among the rows and rows of tulips, hyacinths, and lilies and smelling the pungent rich air that even today I equate with spring.

Paul is encouraging the believers to develop strong "roots" in Christ and to be built up in Him. Just as my family took the necessary steps to ensure root growth so the plants could develop to full maturity, so we too must tend to our faith "roots." Roots grow in both the dark and in the light! No matter whether you are facing a difficult time when things seem cold and dark, or whether things feel warm and sunny, our roots need development. They will take in the nutrients from good soil where they are planted. Be purposeful about your time reading the Word of God, praying, and fellowshipping with other believers. When your roots are strong, the whole plant is strong and will bring joy to those who see you blooming.

Praise God You are developing spiritual roots

Delight Strong roots mean strong faith

Rest No matter what season you are in, your roots are being established

Close in Prayer

Teaching Title _____

_____

_____

_____

_____

_____

_____

_____

_____

_____

_____

_____

_____

_____

_____

_____

_____

_____

_____

_____

_____

_____

_____

_____

Teaching Videos Available for free at www.delightinginthelord.com

WEEK 5
COMPLETE IN CHRIST

While at the church in Antioch, Syria, Paul and Barnabas encountered Jewish legalism among the people. The question arose whether newly-converted Gentiles must be circumcised according to the law of Moses in order to be saved. There was a large dispute over the answer; some said it was faith in Jesus plus circumcision that saved you while others said it was just faith alone in Jesus. The church of Antioch finally agreed that Paul and Barnabas should go to Jerusalem to meet with the apostles and elders to discuss the matter and return with an answer. Peter addressed the Jerusalem group saying, "But we believe that through the grace of the Lord Jesus Christ we shall be saved in the same manner as they…therefore I judge that we should not trouble those from among the Gentiles who are turning to God" (Acts 15:11, 19). The answer had been declared, and a letter was sent out to the Gentiles in Antioch, Syria and Cilicia explaining the decision. It would be my (Brenda) guess that the male Gentile believers all breathed a huge sigh of relief when they heard the news!

Paul will use what he learned at that meeting in Jerusalem and apply it in his letter to the church at Colosse. He warns them not to be robbed of their freedom in Christ. Paul does not want them yoked to anything Christ did not intend for them to bear. They were complete through faith alone, and they could enjoy their relationship with Him without any additional manmade rules or regulations.

> WE HAVE THE BLESSED ASSURANCE THAT FAITH ALONE IS ENOUGH TO SAVE US

We too are complete in Christ. We have the blessed assurance that faith alone is enough to save us, and we can enjoy all the fullness of our relationship with Jesus. We don't need rules and regulations to save us, to keep us in right standing with God, or to deny us of the liberties Christ won for us on the cross. It is incredible how the world wants to always add something to the simplicity of the gospel. Our text in Colossians is a great reminder that we have always been complete in Christ and always will be complete in Christ.

RECEIVING GOD'S WORD

Open in Prayer
Read Colossians 2:8–23

EXPERIENCING GOD'S WORD

EXPERIENCE 1: DON'T BE FOOLED

Colossians 2:8–15

1. In Colossians 2:8 Paul gives the believer a warning. What is it?

    a. Read Colossians 2:9. Based on what you have learned thus far in this study, what does the fullness of the Godhead mean?

    b. What does our choice say when we choose philosophy over the fullness of Christ?

2. There is a very important truth found in Colossians 2:10(NKJV). Fill in the blanks below.

"And you are _____ in Him, who is the _____ of all

_____ and power."

    a. What does it mean to "be complete in Christ?" (v.10)

    b. Read Ephesians 1:19–21. How is Christ the head of power and principality?

3. Read Colossians 2:11–15 and answer the following questions:

    a. In verse 11 Paul uses the Jewish requirement of circumcision as an example to reveal a spiritual concept. Jewish males were circumcised as a sign of the Jewish covenant with God in Genesis 17:9–14. Read Deuteronomy 10:16, 30:6, and Romans 2:28–29. What is Paul conveying about circumcision? How is the cross the instrument used to accomplish the work in our hearts? Is bodily circumcision needed? Explain.

DEEPER EXPERIENCE

"It is not necessary for a believer to submit to circumcision because he has already experienced a spiritual circumcision through his identification with Jesus Christ. But there is a contrast here between Jewish circumcision and the believers' spiritual circumcision in Christ:"

Jews	Believers
External surgery	Internal—the heart
Only a part of the body	The whole "body of sins"
Done by hands	Done without hands
No spiritual help in beating sin	Enables them to overcome sin

(Warren Wiersbe, *Be Complete*, p.92)

    b. The words "putting off the body of the sins of the flesh" are used in verse 11. It means "a total breaking away from." Romans 5:12–15 tells us we are born sinners because of the sin of Adam. Read Romans 6:6–7. How was sin done away with or put off?

c. In verses 12–13 Paul references burial, baptism, and resurrection to symbolize the work Christ accomplished while on the earth. How does a believer identify with Jesus' life, death, and resurrection when they participate in water baptism?

DEEPER EXPERIENCE

"Baptism, then, is a graphic illustration, a one-time ordinance that symbolizes to a watching world the believer's identification with Christ in death, burial and resurrection because this is what we share with Christ. He not only died for me but also as me. Because I am a believer, when He died, I died; when He was buried, I was buried; when He arose, I arose. That is the divine operation. This is no mere ritual; it is the glorious reality. The ordinance simply but graphically portrays it." (John Philips, Exploring Colossians and Philemon, p.125–126.)

d. According to verse 12, how does faith operate in this identification of verses 12–13?

e. Verse 13 says that in Christ we are "made alive together with Him." Read Romans 6:1–5. How do these verses give understanding to Colossians 2:13? How are we dead but alive?

f. Verses 14–15 describe what was accomplished when Jesus died on the cross. What happened and what was accomplished? What was made into a spectacle?

EXPERIENCE 2: BE FREE!

Colossians 2:16–23

1. Read Colossians 2:16–17. How were the false teachers trying to rob the believers of their joy and freedom in Christ? How were they judging the believers' righteousness?

    a. Read Galatians 4:9–11 and 5:1. How does Paul verbalize these same instructions to the church in Galatia? What point is he making?

DEEPER EXPERIENCE

"The law is but a shadow; but in Christ we have the reality, the substance, 'The law is only a shadow of the good things that are coming' (Heb. 10:1 NIV). Why go back into the shadows when we have the reality in Jesus Christ?"
(Warren Wiersbe, Be Complete, p. 102)

2. Read Colossians 2:18 and 1 Corinthians 3:12–15. What warning is Paul giving?

3. Read Colossians 2:19. What is the source of spiritual vitality for God's people? What does it accomplish?

4. Paul is speaking directly to the false teaching of asceticism in verses 20–23. Just to refresh your memory, asceticism is the false teaching of following manmade rules to gain favor with God. The body for the ascetics was something to be punished like an enemy. Why does this go against everything Christ represents?

   a. Based on Colossians 2:23, why would asceticism be alluring? How is pride involved?

5. Read Mark 7:1–8. In these verses Jesus is rebuking the Pharisees for the very thing that Paul is teaching in Colossians 2:20–23. What was Jesus' rebuke?

ACTING ON GOD'S WORD

In Colossians 2:8–23 Paul challenged the believers in Colosse to keep their focus on Jesus. False teachers, philosophy, Judaism, and a variety of belief systems were threatening the life of freedom that the believers were given through Jesus. Paul knew these worldly philosophies were being combined with the gospel and were cheating the believers of the fullness of Christ. He warned the church at Colosse not to follow any belief system that does not conform to a proper knowledge of Christ. We have these same warnings today.

1. How have you seen false religions, cults, and philosophies cheat or rob God's people of the life intended for them through Christ Jesus?

2. Can you identify any false religions today? How do they deny Christ, add to the gospel, or take away from the gospel?

3. Legalism is a trap used by the enemy. It is often subtle. What is legalism? How is it dangerous?

4. Have you ever experienced a legalistic mindset or set of beliefs? Explain.

In this digital age we have access to information unlike any other time in history. Whereas this access can be used by God to spread the gospel, it can also be used by Satan to pull you away from truth. There are many teachers, studies, books, podcasts, and other materials that appear to be Biblically accurate while compromising or promoting a false belief system. We encourage you to be very careful with your information sources. There is a website called www.truthnet.com. When in doubt, this website does a great job of staying on top of movements within the church.

DELIGHTING IN GOD'S WORD DEVOTIONAL

"For in Him dwells all the fullness of the Godhead bodily; and you are complete in Him, who is the head of all principality and power."
Colossians 2:9–10

As far back as I (Stacy) can remember, my mom had the most beautiful perennial flower beds adorning our yards. She loved gardening and even more loved picking the exquisite, often uncommon perennials and tending to them with great care. She paid close attention to all the planting variables and needs of each flower and would fill the flower bed with a variety of colors, textures, and blooming seasons.

As much as she focused on the planting needs, my mom made sure she had the necessary tools to care for each plant. Her gardening bag was the plant's lifeline. Over the years, she taught me about having the right tool for each gardening need. She showed me quality gardening tools, how each one worked, and the importance of keeping them all together in a gardening bag. Even when my daughter, Faith, took an interest in gardening a few years back, my mom bought Faith her very own starter bag and tools.

As the gardener, each tool has a specific purpose for tending the garden. The pruning shears cut off the dead blooms and branches, the trowel digs the soil, the weeder gets to the root of the weed seeking to choke out the plant, and the rake removes the debris that lays on the surface of the garden bed. Of course, no gardener is complete without a watering can which offers the plant one of the very essentials of life. All that a plant needs outside of creation is found in the gardener's bag of tools.

In Colossians 2:9–10 we learned that in Christ we have all we need. We are complete in Christ as the fullness of God lives in Him. When our lives are planted in Christ, He gives us all of Him. He pulls from His boundless bag of resources to help us grow more into His image by using the many tools He has within Himself. In Christ, we are made complete having everything we need for life: He cuts away what is dead, digs up places of our hearts, rakes away the debris, and weeds out sin all while watering us with His life-giving, life-sustaining living water. The life hidden in Christ is truly complete in Christ.

Praise God for loving us enough to give us Jesus.

Delight in the many ways Christ completes you.

Rest in the magnificent, purposeful ways of the Almighty Gardener.

Close in Prayer

Teaching Title _____

_____

_____

_____

_____

_____

_____

_____

_____

_____

_____

_____

_____

_____

_____

_____

_____

_____

_____

_____

_____

_____

_____

_____

_____

Teaching Videos Available for free at www.delightinginthelord.com

WEEK 6
HIDDEN IN CHRIST

Paul, Silas, Timothy, and Luke were on another missionary journey traveling through Philippi. They shared the gospel of Jesus Christ with all who would hear. One day, they joined a group of people gathering for prayer on the outskirts of the city. Lydia and her household were among those eager to hear all that these men had to say about Jesus. God opened her heart to His Truth and her whole household put their faith in Jesus. Later that day their faith was made known by being baptized. With a grateful heart, Lydia invited Paul and his companions to stay at her house while they were in Philippi.

The next day Paul and Silas left Lydia's house to go to another prayer meeting. As they walked through the city streets, a slave girl followed them around while crying out in a loud voice, "These men are servants of the Most-High God, who proclaim to us the way of salvation" (Acts 16:17). She wasn't just any girl. She was known in the town for her divination. She was possessed with a demon and enslaved by masters who made her tell fortunes for their profit. For days she followed Paul and Silas while yelling after them. Paul knew her pratting threatened the truth and authority of his message. Acts 16:18 says, "Paul, greatly annoyed, turned and said to the spirit, 'I command you in the name of Jesus Christ to come out of her.'"

In that moment, beautiful freedom came to that girl. Her torment was gone but so was her masters' source of income. In their anger, they seized Paul and Silas. They dragged them to the authorities, accusing them of disrupting the city as well as being Jews in a primarily Gentile city. The city magistrates agreed and had the men beaten and thrown in prison under close watch by a prison guard.

> FOR ANYONE WHO HAS PUT THEIR FAITH IN JESUS, THEIR LIFE IS NOW HIDDEN IN CHRIST.

The long day eventually turned to night as Paul and Silas sat in a dark, cavern-like prison cell. With aching bodies, bruised and bloody from the beatings, and unable to move as their ankles were held in place by stocks, a song and prayer rose in their hearts. As it flowed out of their mouths for all to hear, the prison was filled with the unusual sound of worship.

How does someone sing praises to God in such a dire situation? As darkness enveloped them, pain ensued, but Paul and Silas still praised God. No darkness could hide the light of Christ that was deep in their souls. No physical pain could overpower the presence of Christ in them. No shackles could hold down a song of worship from rising up in them. In them was hidden all the power and glory of Jesus Christ. Jesus was their hope. Jesus was their future, and their life was secure in Him. The life of Christ was working in them and bringing forth worship, even in the deathly stench of that Philippian prison.

Paul writes about this hidden life in Christ in Colossians 3:1–11. Having set the theological foundation in the previous chapters of Christ's preeminence over creation, His authority in heaven and earth, and His finished work of salvation on the cross, Paul now talks about the life we must live in Christ Jesus because of all these things. We live intimately connected with God through Jesus Christ. Christ is our new identity, and what is His, is also ours by faith.

Paul is personally acquainted with this new life. He remembers his old life before Christ when he persecuted Christians. But after putting his faith in Jesus, Paul began preaching Christ to the very ones he had been persecuting. He knows what it was like to be defined by things of this world one day, and the next day to be defined by Jesus Christ. All the things Paul once held as precious in this world now mean nothing to him; his position, his education, his heritage. All that matters now is his new life in Jesus Christ. So, he sets his mind on Christ by taking his eyes off of the things of this world. Even in that Philippian prison, his mind was set on Jesus. The prison bars couldn't keep Jesus out. His mouth sang from the truths that weren't just lofty ideas about a man but were life-changing truths about his Savior, Jesus Christ, who lived in him.

We, too, must make an ongoing decision, despite our circumstances, to set our minds on Christ and walk in the new life that Jesus Christ offers us. For anyone who has put their faith in Jesus, their life is now hidden in Christ. All that is His is yours for the taking. The appetites and immoralities of this world must be put to death as we walk in the new life Christ offers. We have a responsibility to put off sin and worldliness and to put on the beautiful life of Christ. It is the hidden life of Christ that puts a song in our soul, a prayer of thanks in our hearts, and gives us power to overcome even the darkest prison cells.

RECEIVING GOD'S WORD

Open in Prayer
Read Colossians 3:1–11

EXPERIENCING GOD'S WORD

EXPERIENCE 1: SETTING YOUR MIND ABOVE

Colossians 3:1–4

1. Read Colossians 3:1. The verse has an "if, then" clause. Some versions may say, "Since, then." Who is Paul referring to by saying, "If or since?" What action should then follow for those people? Why?

2. Paul mentions Jesus Christ is seated at the right hand of God in verse 1. Read the following verses and note what you learn about Jesus and heaven.

   Mark 16:19

   Romans 8:34

   Hebrews 12:2

3. Describe the contrast that is being presented in Colossians 3:2. As you do, consider that the word "mind" refers to our will, affections, and devotion, and that the word "set" implies a decisive action.

   a. How does this contrast support what Paul was saying in Colossians 2:16–23 about how the false teachers were deceiving the believers?

4. Read Colossians 3:3. Explain what Paul means when he refers to death and life in this verse. Is it literal or figurative?

    a. Look carefully at the tenses being used with the words "death and life" in verse 3. What has already happened for the believer, and what is our present reality? Why is this distinction an important truth for believers to remember?

    b. Read Romans 6:1–8. We looked at these verses last week as well. Let's look at these verses again but in the context of being dead to sin and alive in Christ. How are we united in Christ? What does that mean about the old life you lived before you asked Jesus to be your Savior?

    c. Read 2 Corinthians 5:17 and Galatians 2:20 which speak of the believer's new life. What does it say about death and life?

d. In Colossians 3:3 the word "life" is the Greek word zoe (G2222). It speaks to the quality of life for the believer. How is the quality of life changed for the believer when they are hidden in Christ?

DEEPER EXPERIENCE

"...and so our lives are indeed 'hidden with Christ in God.' This suggests not only that our lives are secure, but also that they belong in a real and profound sense to the invisible spiritual realm. At the present time our connection with God and Christ is a matter of inner experience; [and outward action], one day it will come into full and open manifestation." (Expositor's Bible Commentary (Abridged Edition):New Testament, by Kenneth L. Barker.)

5. Colossians 3:4 gives us another motivation for seeking those things which are above. Describe this motivation.

a. Read 1 Thessalonians 4:16–18. Describe what it looks like when Christ appears to the church and when we will be glorified.

b. 1 Corinthians 15:42–55 also speaks about the glorified state of the believers. List all that you learn from these verses. How is this worth setting our minds on?

EXPERIENCE 2: TAKE OFF OLD BEHAVIORS

Colossians 3:5–11

1. Read Colossians 3:5. The behaviors from 3:5 are listed in the chart below. Paul tells the believer to put to death these behaviors. Describe what each word means in your own words.

Behaviors from 3:5	Describe in your own words
Fornication	
Uncleanness	
Passion	
Evil desire	
Covetousness	
Idolatry	

   a. Write down any observations you see in these behaviors.

2. Paul tells us in Colossians 3:6 that there is a judgment coming for those who practice disobedience (are rebellious). According to Revelation 22:12–15, when will this happen? Describe the scene.

3. The wrath of God can be a hard concept for some to receive. Let's see what the Bible says about it. Read John 3:36 and Romans 1:18–25. Who are the sons of disobedience described in Colossians and seen in these additional verses? Why will they receive God's wrath?

4. Read Romans 6:23. What consequence does sin demand? What gift did God give to counter this consequence for those who believe in Christ?

5. Read Colossians 3:5–7. How did the Colossians once walk?

   a. Read Colossians 2:6 and contrast this verse with 3:7. Explain the two ways of walking Paul is describing. Which one honors Christ? Why?

6. There is an analogy Paul uses in Colossians 3:8–14. It is the idea of taking off one thing and putting on another. However, in our lesson this week we will only discuss what Paul tells us to "take off." In the next lesson (Week 7) we will examine what Paul recommends we should "put on." Read Colossians 3:8–9a. Fill in the chart below with the behaviors we should "put off" and then describe these behaviors in your own words.

Behavior to Take Off (Old Man)	Describe this behavior in your own words. Use synonyms if needed to effectively communicate what each means to you.
1.	
2.	
3.	
4.	
5.	
6.	

7. From the chart, list any observations you see with the behaviors from verses 5–9.

8. Read Colossians 3:10. How does Paul describe the "new man" and the characteristics that we are to put on?

   a. Read Romans 12:2. How is the new man (woman) in Christ renewed?

9. Read Colossians 3:11. Who can put off the old man and put on the new man? Is there partiality or prejudice with God?

   a. Why is it significant that Paul would give these appeals after he already reminded the believers of the gospel and explained what a believer's life in Christ should look like because of the gospel in chapters 1–2 of Colossians?

ACTING ON GOD'S WORD

In our lesson the believer was given four commands to follow. Because we have been given a new life in Christ, we are commanded to live a new life through Him. He gives us all we need in order to be obedient to these commands. We learned that our spiritual life holds a different quality than the natural or earthly life we were familiar with before putting our faith in Jesus. Paul made a strong contrast between earthly and spiritual life, as well as spiritual death and spiritual life. Let's look at the four commands he gave and apply them to our lives.

1. *"Seek those things which are above." Colossians 3:1*
   a. What do you find yourself seeking in this world that might take your focus off of Jesus?

   b. What does it mean for you personally to seek things that are above, especially in times of difficult circumstances? How can you, practically speaking, know when you are doing this?

2. *"Set your mind on things above" Colossians 3:2*
   The National Science Foundation says that a person has between 12,000–60,000 thoughts per day. Of those, 80% are negative and an astonishing 95% are repetitive. Let's consider this for a moment.

   a. What was the last thought that went through your mind?

b. What was the last negative thought that went through your mind?

c. What was the last repetitive thought that went through your mind?

d. Based on what you learned today, how is it possible for this statistic to be different for a believer?

3. *"Put to death your members which are on the earth"* Colossians 3:5

   a. Look at the list of sins that Paul says should be put to death. They are listed below. Check any that are still evident in your life or any area of struggle.

   __fornication/sexual immorality

   __Impurity/uncleanness

   __Lust/sinful passions

   __Evil desires

   __Covetousness/greed/idolatry

b. Paul shares that these sins should not characterize our life, so much so that he refers to them as "needing to die." That means these actions have no breath, movement, sustenance, or ability in our new spiritual life. This is possible through the work of the Holy Spirit and our obedience to Him. Spend a few minutes in prayer. Confess the sin before God. Ask for His forgiveness and His power to put this sin to death.

4. **"Since you have *put off* the old man with his deeds, and have *put on* the new man..."**
    Colossians 3:9–10
    Paul uses the picture of taking off old, sinful behaviors and putting on Christ-like behaviors. This can be likened to how we dress and undress each day. Paul gives us a two-part command. We are to fight sin and walk in holiness. Do you spend too much time fighting and not enough time pursuing holiness? What results if we spend too much time in one of these areas while neglecting the other?

"Therefore, put to death your members which are on the earth: fornication, uncleanness, passion, evil desire, and covetousness, which is idolatry. Because of these things the wrath of God is coming upon the sons of disobedience, in which you yourselves once walked when you lived in them."

Colossians 3:5–7

My (Brenda's) mom, Carrie, is an avid gardener. Her yard is well groomed and maintained. Throughout the growing months in Pennsylvania, she nearly always has some unique plant blossoming in her yard which brings special beauty to her property. She has been especially fond of her iris plants which came from her mother's home in Michigan, and for many years they were just exquisite. Then one spring, when the foliage began to develop, it looked sickly, and it quickly became apparent something was wrong. Upon deeper investigation, she realized the rhizomes (which look a bit like a bulb) were under attack. Normally, rhizomes are firm and clean, but hers were full of holes and mushy. Being a diligent gardener, Mom dug them up, cut off their tops, and soaked them in a chemical solution her local greenhouse recommended to kill the worms that were eating her iris. Further, she contacted the Pennsylvania Horticultural Society, and after explaining what had happened, they recommended that she purchase some nematodes (round worms) and place them in the soil because they are the natural enemy to the iris borer. Even after the treatment to the rhizomes and amending the soil with nematodes, the iris have never returned to their original glory.

This story reminds me a bit of our text from Colossians 3:5–7. We are encouraged to put to death those things that are harmful to us and are sins against God. They, like the worms in my mom's iris plants, must be removed. We cannot just hope the sin will stop or remove just some of the sinful things we are doing; rather, Paul says we must literally kill all of it. We must take all the necessary steps to both kill the "worms" (sin) and also take care of the "soil" (our heart). Sin often has a way of leaving a mark upon us so avoiding it all together is the best practice. However, if we find ourselves entrenched in wrongdoing, asking God to forgive us and turning from it will make us clean and healthy once again.

Praise God we don't have to walk in our sinful ways, we can put them to death because of Christ.

Delight in God's forgiveness for our sins.

Rest in God's cleansing and the fresh start He makes available every day.

Close in Prayer

Teaching Title _____

_____

_____

_____

_____

_____

_____

_____

_____

_____

_____

_____

_____

_____

_____

_____

_____

_____

_____

_____

_____

_____

_____

_____

_____

_____

Teaching Videos Available for free at www.delightinginthelord.com

WEEK 7
DRESSED IN CHRIST

Despite the pain from their beatings and the stocks around their feet, Paul and Silas were praying and singing hymns to God from their Philippian prison cell (Acts 16:25). These two men demonstrated such unusual behaviors that I (Brenda) must assume they were a rare sight and sound in such a hostile place. As midnight came, they lifted their voices to the One they knew could save them. Maybe they sang to encourage one another; however, there were others around them listening. Paul and Silas were different, and their actions demonstrated that their hope came from somewhere beyond themselves. They chose to worship and trust God even when their circumstances were dark, distressing, and difficult.

And then the earth began to shake. Perhaps they were interrupted in the middle of their hymn when the earthquake tremors began. Maybe the shaking was subtle initially before it became so intense that it broke open the prison doors and the chains fell from the prisoners' legs. However, when the prison keeper became aware of what had occurred, he feared the worst. Under Roman law, if prisoners escaped, he would be held responsible for their disappearance and put to death. Because the jailer thought the men had already fled, he drew his sword to kill himself, but Paul cried out telling him not to harm himself because they were all present in the prison.

> LET US CLOTHE OURSELVES IN THE CHARACTER TRAITS OF CHRIST, THROUGH THE POWER OF THE HOLY SPIRIT, SO THAT HE MAY BE GLORIFIED IN AND THROUGH US.

What unfolded next must have been an intense few moments! Can you imagine the jailer's face as he called for a torch and scanned the room to be sure everyone was still detained? I can picture his eyes straining and perhaps counting out loud as he tallied up the men, but once he realized they were all present and accounted for, he fell at the feet of Paul asking what he must do to be saved.

The details regarding how the jailer knew Paul and Silas could tell him how to be saved are not explained for us in Acts 16. My guess is that their legacy had preceded them, and their conduct confirmed what the jailer had heard about them was indeed true. These men were not his typical prisoners, and they did not serve a typical God. But, regardless of what the jailer knew previously, when he asked how to be saved, Paul and Silas told him it was simply done by putting his faith in Jesus Christ. Then without delay, in the middle of the night, the jailer and his whole family became believers.

I cannot help but wonder if this incredible night was in the back of Paul's mind when he wrote Colossians 3:12–17. He encourages the church at Colosse to behave in a Christ-like manner and mentions specifically to be merciful, kind, humble, meek, longsuffering, loving, peaceful, and forgiving so that the fullness of Christ can dwell in them. When the fullness of Christ dwells in us, others often take notice just like the jailer did in the Philippian jail.

When we live in the power of the Holy Spirit, it is possible to sing when we are sad, offer hope when we are in distress, forgive when we want to harbor a debt, be grateful when we want to be resentful, and be humble when we want to boast. When this is the consistent way we live, we will be noticed because it is the opposite of how most of the world behaves. There may be opposition to our message of hope and love, but there will be others who, because of our actions, will turn and say, "What must I do to be saved?" Let us clothe ourselves in the character traits of Christ, through the power of the Holy Spirit, so that He may be glorified in and through us.

RECEIVING GOD'S WORD

Open in Prayer
Read Colossians 3:12–17

EXPERIENCING GOD'S WORD

EXPERIENCE 1: CHOSEN, HOLY & LOVED

Colossians 3:12

1. Read Colossians 3:12. The first word in this verse is "Therefore." Whenever we read this word in Scripture, it should prompt us to look back over the previous verses to understand what is being said next. Re-read Colossians 3:1–11 and summarize our new life in Christ and what you've learned about our obedience as a result of this life.

2. In Colossians 3:12 Paul uses three words to describe the believer: the elect, holy, and beloved (NKJV). Let's look into this description.

    Elect: (Strong's G1588) means to be picked out, chosen by God through salvation in Christ. Christians are called the chosen or the elect of God.

    a. Read Ephesians 1:3–6. How does Paul use these verses in Ephesians to reinforce the spiritual truth about election found in Colossians 3:12? Describe all the blessings that result.

DEEPER EXPERIENCE

Election can sometimes sidetrack people regarding God's plan and who can be saved. To keep things simple, remember Jesus died for the sins of the whole world (John 3:16). We've already learned in Colossians that you have a choice to make regarding Jesus Christ. Anyone can be a part of God's election if they choose to put their faith in Jesus as their Lord and Savior.

    Holy: (Strong's G40) means to be separated from sin; therefore, consecrated to God, sacred.

    a. Read 1 Peter 1:15. How does Peter explain our holiness?

    Beloved: (Strong's G25) means to love selflessly in a social or moral sense, to regard with strong affection.

    a. Read 1 John 4:9–11. What do these verses say about God's love for us? Why does He call us beloved?

3. Last week we looked at Romans 12:2 regarding our minds. Look at this verse again. Use Colossians 3:12 and Romans 12:2 to explain why our lives should be a reflection of Christ.

4. Paul uses the rest of this section to talk about the clothing of Christ we are to put on. Read Colossians 3:12–17. Paul gives a list of behaviors and Christ-like attributes that should be evident in the life of a believer. Using the chart below, in your own words describe the behaviors and attributes found in these verses that Paul tells us to "put on."

Behavior to Put On (New Man)	Describe this behavior in your own words. Use synonyms if needed to effectively communicate what each means to you.
Tender mercies/ Compassion	
Kindness	
Humility	
Meekness/Gentleness	
Long suffering/Patience	
Bearing with one another	
Forgiveness	
Love	

continued

Behavior to Put On (New Man)	Describe this behavior in your own words. Use synonyms if needed to effectively communicate what each means to you.
Peace	
Thankfulness	
Wisdom	
Teaching	
Admonishing	

5. In Week 2 of this study we had you look at the fruit of the Spirit listed in Galatians 5:22–23. Much of the fruit listed in Galatians is seen in Colossians 3:12–17. This fruit comes from a Spirit-filled life. Read Galatians 5:16–18. How is it possible to *"put on"* the Spirit-filled life in Christ?

a. Look back at your answer for question 1 of this lesson. It is not within our sin nature (old self) to exhibit these qualities. Based on all you've learned so far, how is it possible to *exhibit* Christ's character by putting on the virtues found in Colossians 3:12–17?

EXPERIENCE 2: PUT ON THE VIRTUES OF CHRIST

Colossians 3:12–14

1. Compassion, kindness, humility, and meekness are the first set of Christ-like character qualities Paul says to put on in Colossians 3:12. Look up the following verses that speak about Christ's interactions with people. What qualities do you see Him portraying in these verses? Describe how Jesus is demonstrating these qualities.

   Matthew 9:35–38

   John 4:1–26

   John 13:3–17

2. Long suffering/patience, bearing with one another, and forgiveness are the second set of Christ-like character qualities. Read Colossians 3:12b–13. Look up the following verses that speak about Christ's interactions with people. What qualities do you see Him portraying in these verses? Describe how Jesus is demonstrating these qualities.

   Matthew 17:17–23

   John 13:36–38, John 21:15–19

   Luke 23:32–46

3. Love is the third attribute of having a Christ-like character. Read Colossians 3:14. Look up the following verses that speak about Christ's interactions with people. What qualities do you see Him portraying in these verses? Describe how Jesus is demonstrating these qualities.

John 3:16

John 15:9–17

4. You already looked at 1 Corinthians 13:1–13 in Week 2 of this study. Go back and read your answer to this question. We asked you to describe Christ-like love from these verses. Reread the verses if you need to refresh your memory. Why is love the greatest Christ-like quality we need to choose to demonstrate?

a. In Colossians 3:14 love is described as the bond of perfection. The NLT version of the Bible states the verse this way: "Above all clothe yourselves with love, which binds us all together in perfect harmony." Why is love elevated above all the other virtues listed so far? Why is this significant?

EXPERIENCE 3: ADORNED IN PEACE AND TRUTH

Colossians 3:15–17

1. Read Colossians 3:15–16. In these verses Paul switches from using the words "put on" to the word "let." According to dictionary.com, the word "let" means to allow or not to prohibit. Fill in the blanks below from verse 15–16. We used the NKJV.

   V. 15: Let the _____ of _____ _____
   in your hearts

   V. 16: Let the _____ of _____ _____ in you richly.

2. Let's look at the peace of God from Colossians 3:16. Read the following verses and note what you learn about the peace of God.

   John 14:27

   Philippians 4:6–7

   Isaiah 26:3–4

3. The word "rule" found in Colossians 3:15 is the word *brabeuō* (G1018) which means to act like an umpire, arbitrate, or to decide. Given this definition, how should we allow the peace of God to decide or be the umpire concerning matters of our hearts?

   a. In verse 15 Paul stresses the importance of allowing the peace of God to rule us individually, but he also extends it to relationships, specifically within the body of Christ. How does the peace of God bring about unity in relationships?

b. What attitude does Paul add at the end of verse 15? How is this attitude an outcropping of the peace of God?

4. In Colossians 3:16 Paul encourages us to let the Word of God (Christ) dwell in us richly. Explain how the Word of Christ lives in believers.

5. From verse 16, what does the Word of God (Christ) produce when it lives in the heart of a believer?

a. How does the Word of God affect relationships as well?

b. Paul encourages us to worship in Colossians 3:16. Read 1 Timothy 3:16. Here Paul writes the lyrics to an early church hymn. Why would singing this hymn, or something like it, encourage the church at Colosse?

6. Read Colossians 3:17. When we speak (words) and do things (deeds), who should we be looking to please? How should gratitude be involved in words and deeds?

   a. Read Matthew 6:1–4. What warning does Jesus give regarding service in His name?

   b. As Jesus is our ultimate example, read John 14:31 and 17:1–5. How did Jesus exemplify Colossians 3:17 and leave us an example to follow?

ACTING ON GOD'S WORD

"And whatever you do in word or deed, do all in the name of the Lord Jesus, giving thanks to God the Father through Him." Colossians 3:17

Throughout Colossians 3:1–17 Paul gave eleven behaviors to avoid and eleven behaviors to imitate. If we had to boil all seventeen verses down into one, Colossians 3:17 captures the essence of them all by reminding us that whatever we do, it should all be done in the name of the Lord Jesus. That may seem like a tough command considering that many people we interact with may not want to even hear the name Jesus, let alone have our actions be done in His name. So, how is it possible to do what Paul is suggesting? I (Brenda) believe it comes down to our relationship with Christ and not a set of rules to follow. If we aim to love Christ and not sin against Him, then we are much more likely to love and treat others as He desires.

1. Colossians 3:17 says, "Whatever you do in word or deed, do all in the name of the Lord Jesus." What does it mean to do something in the name of the Lord Jesus? List some of your "alls" in life below and then describe how those actions or responsibilities could be done in the name of the Lord Jesus.

2. The same verse speaks of our words honoring God. What do God-honoring words look like? What don't they look like?

   a. Think about your relationships for a moment. Choose one relationship you wish was better. What can you apply from Colossians 3:12–17 to help make your words more honoring in this specific relationship? What result might you see over time?

3. Paul encourages his reader to "give thanks to God" in the latter part of Colossians 3:17; however, sometimes this can be difficult with people who do not believe in Christ. Consider the following scenarios and give potential solutions of ways to glorify God and be grateful.

a. You are out to dinner and you want to thank God for the meal, but you are not sure how to initiate the blessing.

b. You have received an unexpected answer to prayer but are not sure how to praise God because your unsaved family member has shared the news.

c. You demonstrated great restraint and gave someone the benefit of the doubt when everyone else around you was bashing a colleague. You want to tell them that it was a work of the Lord in you. How can you express it without seeming superior?

"Therefore, as the elect of God, holy and beloved,
put on tender mercies, kindness, humility,
meekness, longsuffering;"
Colossians 3:12

I (Stacy) would never describe myself as having a green thumb. I enjoy planting shrubs along our landscape, and love using bushes and greenery to add texture and variation. Flowers are not my forte; however, there is one exception, the massive hydrangea bush that flanks the side of my yard. It is one of my favorite flowers, rivaling the tulip. I can't take credit for the magnificent flowering bush. It was planted long before we moved into our house. It has such deep roots that it has given me an abundance of fresh cut hydrangeas each season, even more than enough to share with my other hydrangea-loving friends.

Each year in late spring I anxiously await the bush's lush leaves to give way to the delicate hydrangea blooms. The blooms are always a light blue mixed with white; graceful in appearance and understated in their display. Despite their delicate form, they are strong in fortitude, weathering many winters and coming back even larger with each new spring season. Hummingbirds are attracted to the full clusters as are the cardinals who find cover under the broad leaves and the songbirds who love the seeds. The beauty of the hydrangea speaks for itself giving any garden bed a beautiful array.

In Colossians 3:12 Paul talks to believers about their Christ-like character. For those rooted in Christ, He tells us our lives must display His character and qualities. Our lives, both in word and action, should burst with Christ's glorious array of beauty. Like the hydrangea bush offering cuttings for others to enjoy, so should our lives be ones that others desire to be around and share. Even as the hydrangea bush both attracts and protects those birds who visit, we, too, should be a safe place for others as we offer them the love and kindness that is Christ's. We will go through many winters, but clothed in Christ we know that spring will always come. And following the harshest of winters comes the most beautiful blooms.

Praise God for the beauty of Christ's character that is given to us.

Delight in His grace, love, meekness, and longsuffering.

Rest in His arms and take comfort in His embrace.

Close in Prayer

Teaching Title _____

_____

_____

_____

_____

_____

_____

_____

_____

_____

_____

_____

_____

_____

_____

_____

_____

_____

_____

_____

_____

_____

Teaching Videos Available for free at www.delightinginthelord.com

WEEK 8
RELATIONSHIPS ESTABLISHED IN CHRIST

If there was ever someone in the Bible who knew about relationships, it would certainly be the apostle Paul. An often-overlooked aspect of his ministry is the many relationships he established through church planting and following God's call into missions. Throughout his 30 years of ministry, many connections were formed; close ones were tested, disagreements happened, and yet, God was put first and honored. While traveling to each city to share the gospel, as well as through the people he cared about in his own life, Paul saw first-hand the beauty and pain of interpersonal relationships.

But it seems Paul's love for people came only after his love for God's Son was first established. When Paul put his faith in Jesus on the Damascus Road, he tells us in Galatians 1:17 that he first went to the Arabian Desert for three years before he started preaching Christ in Jerusalem and beyond. Paul doesn't tell us about his time in Arabia so it is hard to know both the reason he was there as well as what he did during those three years. What we do know from Acts 9:29 is that when Paul arrived in Jerusalem, three years after becoming a believer in Jesus Christ, he spoke boldly in the name of Jesus Christ. A transformation had happened within him that became evident to all who interacted with him. Was the Arabian Desert a training ground much like it was for Moses in Midian, Elijah in the wilderness, and even Jesus Himself when He was led to the desert for a time of testing?

> JESUS IS OVER ALL THINGS, INCLUDING RELATIONSHIPS. HE CREATED RELATIONSHIPS, ORDERED THEM, AND HAS A DESIGN FOR EACH ONE.

One could infer that during this time in Arabia, Paul's relationship with God through Jesus Christ became deeply rooted, established, and built up; so much so that in some of Paul's letters to God's people he would call himself a bondservant of Jesus Christ. Having received the gospel directly from God, not from man, Paul learned quickly that the most important relationship is always with Jesus. It is through Him that everything else in life flows and everything must function. Jesus is over all things, including relationships. He created relationships, ordered them, and has a design for each one.

In Colossians 3:18–4:1 Paul gives very direct and poignant commands for marriage and parenting, as well as for connections in the work world. Scripture makes no mention of Paul being married. He refers to himself in 1 Corinthians 7:8 as being unmarried. And yet, throughout his writings, he teaches husbands, wives, and parents. How does he do this? He does it under the Holy Spirit's guidance as he says in 1 Corinthians 7:10 to those who are married, "I command, yet not I but the Lord..."

It is with this in mind that I (Stacy) encourage you to go into these verses found in Colossians with a soft and open heart to hear all that the Holy Spirit wants to speak to you. Take a moment and pray. Ask God to prepare your heart and to work His truths into the places of your marriage, your parenting, and/or work relationships where there is possibly a halt in your flesh based on worldly teaching. God's order and design often goes against the world's order and design.

Keep in mind that the context for these verses in Colossians 3:18–4:1 comes from the preceding verses, especially 3:16 which says, "Let the Word of Christ dwell in you richly in all wisdom...." His Word challenges our thinking and demands something from us. If we choose to come under the authority of His Word, we must come under the authority of all His Word. We can't pick and choose what we want to follow and what we don't.

It is from Christ's indwelling Spirit and the living Word that we are able to carry out God's commands found in these verses. I am praying for you as I write these words that you would allow God's instruction in the area of relationships to reorder, restore, bring repentance, if needed, and above all, be redemptive in your marriages, parenting, and work relationships.

RECEIVING GOD'S WORD

Open in Prayer
Read Colossians 3:18–4:1

EXPERIENCING GOD'S WORD

EXPERIENCE 1: HUSBAND AND WIFE RELATIONSHIP

Colossians 3:18–19

1. Read Colossians 3:18. Fill in the blank below.

   Wives _____ to your own husband, as is fitting in the Lord.

   a. In your own words define *submit*. What synonyms come to mind when you think of this word?

2. Before looking at submission in a marriage relationship, let's first look at the Godhead (God, Jesus Christ, and Holy Spirit) as our example of submission. Read the verses below and note how Christ submits to God the Father.

    John 6:38

    1 Corinthians 11:3

    Philippians 2:5–8

3. Read Colossians 2:9–10. You've previously studied these verses. There is both hierarchy and oneness within the Godhead. Read Genesis 2:21–24. What do you learn about the first marriage relationship regarding hierarchy and oneness?

    a. From the verses in Genesis, what do you notice about the creation of the woman? What bone did God use from Adam to create the woman? Think about this bone in regard to all the other bones God could have used. What is meaningful about this bone when thinking about oneness and submission in the husband/wife relationship?

4. God is a God of order and submission. Read the following verses and briefly summarize the submission and order seen in creation, government, the church, and relationships.

   Creation: Genesis 1–2:3

   Government: Romans 13:1–7

   Church: 1 Corinthians 14:26–33, 40

   Relationships: Ephesians 5:17–21

5. Based on what you just learned about the Godhead and the order He created, hopefully you've seen how submission is woven into all areas of life. The word "submit" is the Greek word *hypotasso* (G5293). Vines Dictionary defines this word as a military term meaning, "to rank under someone else or to put yourself under someone's authority." As wives, we are instructed to "submit" to our husbands. How does the definition help you understand God's command and your responsibility as a wife?

6. Read James 4:7. Why is this the first relationship in which you must understand submission before you can properly submit in any other relationship?

7. Read Ephesians 5:22 and Colossians 3:18. Fill in the blank.

   "Wives submit to your _____ husbands." Why is this important in the marriage relationship? How is this a protection for us as wives?

8. Read Ephesians 5:22–24 and describe the Godly order of marriage from this verse by filling in the diagram.

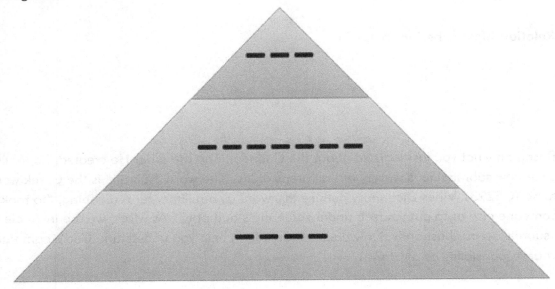

9. Read Genesis 3:16. When Adam and Eve sinned against God, consequences were given to them and all mankind. This verse describes the consequences given to women. How was submission part of the consequences? How does this help you understand why submission to your husband is fundamentally difficult?

DEEPER EXPERIENCE

> *"We cannot have two heads of state in a nation, or we invite civil war. We cannot have two men running a corporation, each holding opposite views. We cannot have two commanders-in-chief of the country's armed forces. And we cannot have two heads of a family. God has ordained the man to be the head of his home. He is not the boss, but he is the head. Moreover, if he abdicates that headship, he does so to the detriment of himself, his wife and his children."*
> *(John Phillips, Exploring Colossians and Philemon, p.190)*

10. Read Colossians 3:19. What two commands are given to husbands?

11. Read Ephesians 5:25–33 and answer the following questions.
    a. How is a husband commanded to love his wife? How did Jesus demonstrate this type of love for the Church?

    b. What is a husband's responsibility to his wife before God?

    c. Describe the oneness of a husband's care for his wife.

    d. How is the love of Christ for the Church an example for the husband to follow?

e.   What does a husband need from his wife?

12. Colossians 3:19 tells a husband not to be bitter toward his wife. How does the wife's respect impact her husband?

13. Read 1 Peter 3:1–6. Once again a wife is commanded to submit to her husband. Based on these verses in 1 Peter, is the submission commandment void when a husband does not uphold his God-given responsibilities or is not a believer? Explain.

DEEPER EXPERIENCE

"Headship is not dictatorship or lordship. It is loving leadership. In fact, both the husband and the wife must be submitted to the Lord and to each other (Eph. 5:21). It is a mutual respect under the lordship of Jesus Christ."(Warren Wiersbe, Be Complete, p. 140).

EXPERIENCE 2: PARENT AND CHILD RELATIONSHIPS

Colossians 3:20–21

1.   Read Colossians 3:20. What command is given to children regarding their parents?

a. Based on what you learned about submission, why would this be pleasing to the Lord?

b. Why would the husband and wife relationship come before the parent and child relationship within God's order?

c. What happens when God's order is not followed?

2. Read Exodus 20:12 and Ephesians 6:2–3. This command is so important that God included it in the Ten Commandments and reiterated it in the New Testament. This command comes with a promise from God. What is that promise?

a. How does fostering obedience in a child's life help them grow into a God-fearing adult?

3. Read Luke 2:41–52. Describe how Jesus submitted to His parents' authority as a young man. In what ways did God reward His obedience?

4. Read Colossians 3:21 and Ephesians 6:4. There are clear instructions given to fathers regarding their children. The Greek word used for *father* can include the mother as well according to the Strong's Concordance definition of *father* (Strong's G3962). What does it mean to provoke a child? How does this negatively affect a child's spiritual development?

a. How does this command to fathers (parents) actually protect children?

b. How should a father (parent) be parenting a child according to this verse? Explain.

DEEPER EXPERIENCE

"If a home is truly Christian, it is a place of encouragement. In such a home, the child finds refuge from battles, and yet strength to fight the battles and carry the burdens of growing maturity. He finds a loving heart, a watching eye, a listening ear, a helping hand. He does not want any other place— home meets his needs. In this kind of a home, it is natural for the child to trust Christ and want to live for Him." (Warren Wiersbe, Be Complete, p. 145).

EXPERIENCE 3: WORKPLACE RELATIONSHIPS

Colossians 3:22–4:1

1. Read Colossians 3:22. Here Paul addresses the relationship between a slave and their master. Whereas slavery is still present in modern day society, thankfully it has been abolished in much of the world and is a relationship that is unfamiliar to most of us. For our purposes in this study we will take the term "slave" and consider it as a type of paid worker or servant. Slaves were considered a working class of people at the time Paul wrote Colossians. Paul gives four commands in this verse which are listed on the following page. Rewrite each command in your own words.

a. Obey in all things your masters according to the flesh

b. Not with eyeservice as men-pleasers

c. But in sincerity of heart

d. Fearing God

e. How do these commands honor God?

DEEPER EXPERIENCE

"Read Paul's little letter to Philemon and see his attitude toward slavery. Paul did not advise Philemon to treat his runaway slave severely, but to receive him as a brother even though he was still a slave. In fact, Onesimus, the slave, was one of the men who carried this letter to Colosse (Col. 4:9)!" (Warren Wiersbe, Be Complete, p. 146)

DEEPER EXPERIENCE

"More than half the people seen on the streets of the great cities of the Roman world were slaves. And this was the status of the majority of 'professional' people such as teachers and doctors as well as that of menials and craftsmen." (Vaughan quoted by David Guzik, www.blueletterbible.org)

2. Read Romans 6:22. It speaks to our relationship with God through Jesus Christ. How are all believers considered slaves?

3. Read 1 Corinthians 6:19–20. How should the truth that God is our Master impact the way we live regarding our relationships?

4. Read Colossians 3:23–24. Paul reminds the church at Colosse who they work for, how their work should be accomplished, and how they will be rewarded for their work. The worldly system teaches us that success comes as we get ahead of others at work and move up the proverbial corporate ladders. God's success for the worker is defined much differently. Compare and contrast the worker who works for worldly success versus the worker who works for spiritual success.

Worldly Worker   **Spirit-filled worker**

5. Read Colossians 3:25. Describe how Paul's concluding remarks would comfort someone who served under an unjust master or convict someone who does not submit to someone in authority over them.

6. In Colossians 4:1 we read about how masters should treat their bondservants. Again, in our society today we could consider the "master" to be like a type of supervisor in a working relationship. What does Paul tell the masters to keep in mind when they are overseeing their servants?

    a. Who are masters accountable to and why should this dictate their behaviors?

ACTING ON GOD'S WORD

EVERYONE

We have learned from Paul's letter to Colosse that there is a God-ordained order for all of life's relationships. This order begins with the Lord as we choose to submit to Him first. From that place of submission, we can more easily submit to each other in every relationship.

1. How does our submission to God affect our desire and ability to submit in our marriages, to our parents, and within our workplaces? Explain

In the verses just studied, we learned about God's design, order, and desire regarding marriage, parenting, and working relationships. When we choose to submit to those God has put in leadership, we are honoring the Lord. I (Brenda) feel it might be easier to apply some of the text we have studied this week if we break this portion of the lesson apart based upon the relationships we studied. If you are married, please answer the questions that fall under the heading "Married." If you aren't married, go to the next relationship heading that applies to you.

MARRIED

We learned Colossians 3:18 says, "Wives submit to your own husbands." However, before we begin to make some applications, I believe it is important to remember what submission is not; submission does not mean being abused.

If you are in an abusive relationship, this is outside God's design, especially in marriage. God commands husbands to love their wives (Col. 3:19). There is help available for those who find themselves in an abusive situation. Please tell your Delighting in the Lord leader or another leader at your church about your circumstances. Additionally, you may want to reach out to the following organizations for help:

- In Chester County, PA the abuse hotline is 888-711-6270.
- The National Domestic Violence Hotline (www.thehotline.org) is 1-800-799-7233.
- If you cannot speak safely, you may text "LOVEIS" to 1-866-331-9474. An advocate who is trained will speak with you confidentially and assist you with resources, information, and answer any questions.

When two people are in a safe marriage relationship, God's design in marriage provides order to the household. Let's explore how this can be done by answering the following questions for those who are married:

1. Is there an area that is difficult for you to allow your husband to lead in your marriage? Explain why.

a. What have you learned about your responsibility in your marriage that is independent of your husband's? How will it honor God and His design?

2. How can a wife be submissive and express her opinion when she and her husband do not agree on a topic or decision? At my husband's workplace they have a phrase that is often used when two people cannot agree on something, and it is, "Disagree and then commit." This phrase does not mean that both parties are always happy about the decision, but ultimately after both sides have been heard, they put aside their differences and together commit to the plan. How can a husband and wife disagree but then together commit to the plan?

PARENTS

1. God's command in Colossians 3:20 is pretty clear regarding a child's and parent's responsibility. A child must obey, and a parent must require obedience as the one in authority. How does your God-given role and responsibility both empower and equip you as a parent as you train your children in the area of obedience?

2. In Colossians 3:20 we are told to not exasperate or provoke our children. In what ways can we do this? How does this undermine our authority as their parents?

WORKING/SERVICE RELATIONSHIPS

1. Are there times you may be tempted to divide your work into two categories: the secular and the sacred? How does Paul's teaching go against this way of thinking?

ALL RELATIONSHIPS

1. How does Colossians 3:18–4:1 encourage you, challenge you, and/or comfort you?

DELIGHTING IN GOD'S WORD DEVOTIONAL

(Eugene, Brenda's dad, in the garden—photo credit Carrie Ferri)

"Wives, submit to your own husbands, as is fitting in the Lord. Husbands, love your wives and do not be bitter toward them. Children, obey your parents in all things, for this is well pleasing to the Lord." Colossians 3:18–20

Throughout my (Brenda) childhood, my parents maintained a large garden. As a family, we all participated in the gardening process, growing many varieties of vegetables. My Dad would organize our family to help assist and cultivate our agricultural endeavor in the backyard. It typically began in the early spring when Dad would get the rototiller out of the shed and run it through the ground where he intended to set the boundaries for the garden. It was a heavy machine, and I remember it terrifying me. It was louder than the lawn mower, and its sharp blades chomping into the ground sent me running to the porch of the house to watch from a safe distance. While my dad was wrangling the beast, which was breaking up the ground, my mom was in the shed gathering the seeds, string, and stakes; all necessary to plant the vegetables. Once my parents completed their tasks, my brother and I were instructed on how to plant the seeds. There was specific spacing needed, depending upon what vegetable we were growing, and the two of us were to place them where Mom had marked out the neat, symmetrical rows.

We all had specific assignments, and when they were accomplished, it made for an orderly garden where growth could occur and eventually a harvest reaped. My dad alone did the rototilling because it was a job only someone very physically strong could tackle. My mom gladly got the other materials necessary to prep the ground so the seeds could be deposited into the soil. My brother and I were obedient to the instructions given to us by our parents because we knew they had experience with growing a garden. Further, we knew that later in the summer, by helping out in the spring, we would enjoy the sweet corn, lettuce, tomatoes, and other vegetables we were planting.

Being a part of the yearly garden project with my family serves as a good example for the truth contained in Colossians 3:18–20. God has given us instructions on how to run a God-honoring household. Each person in the family has been given responsibilities, and when they are done obediently, a harvest of righteousness and peace is produced. If my mom had tried to till the soil with the rototiller, she may have been injured. Because she understood this, she willingly allowed my father to do the job. My brother and I did not have the knowledge needed to choose the seeds that would be best for our garden, so we defaulted to our parents' knowledge and obeyed their instructions. Each member submitted to each other so that the job could be accomplished smoothly.

When we consider how this analogy is similar to our text from Colossians, we should remember that all members of a household benefit when we submit one to another with love. Our actions and attitudes bring glory to God, harmony to the household, and a harvest in due time.

Praise God that He is a good Father who knows what is best for His children.
Delight in the peace that comes from trusting God's orderly instructions.
Rest through submitting to the authority God has given for Christian households.

Close in Prayer

Teaching Title_____

_____

_____

_____

_____

_____

_____

_____

_____

_____

_____

_____

_____

_____

_____

_____

_____

_____

_____

_____

_____

Teaching Videos Available for free at www.delightinginthelord.com

WEEK 9
MINISTERING IN CHRIST

It was toward the end of his third missionary journey when Paul invited the elders from Ephesus to meet him in Miletus (Acts 20:17). There were instructions Paul wanted to give the men before he returned to Jerusalem. Paul knew the importance of ministering in the name of Christ with excellence and diligence. He used himself as an example to teach them how to serve others as he himself had served. He had been a humble, loving, compassionate ambassador for Jesus Christ. He persevered even when he encountered beatings, shipwrecks, persecution, and rejection. Paul allowed the Holy Spirit to be his guide as he shared the gospel and was alert to the schemes of the enemy who wished to rob, kill, and destroy the work he was accomplishing. He was not a financial burden to others and earned an income so he could fulfill God's calling on his life. After encouraging the leadership with these and other reminders, "He knelt down and prayed with them all" (Acts 20:36). The leadership, knowing this would be their last face-to-face encounter with Paul, accompanied him to his ship, and with tears they said good-bye to their co-laborer.

Stacy and I can relate to this account from Paul's life as well as this week's text, Colossians 4:2–18. We try our best to follow the exhortation Paul gave the elders from Ephesus and to the church at Colosse in the way we minister to others. We want to be women who represent Jesus well and draw others into a deeper walk with Him. With every word we speak, every prayer we pray, each event we host, and every study we write, it is our desire to follow the Holy Spirit so we do not hinder the work God is trying to accomplish through us as we minister in His name. To labor for Christ means sometimes saying, "No" to one thing so we can say, "Yes" to a greater thing. This discernment can only be accomplished as we follow the Holy Spirit and ask for His guidance and wisdom. We take what we do at Delighting in the Lord very seriously and hope that our example will be an encouragement to others who lead beside us.

> HE DESIRED THEY WOULD BE DILIGENT IN PRAYER, WAIT ON THE LORD'S DIRECTION, WALK IN WISDOM, SPEAK CAREFULLY, AND ABOUND IN GRACE.

Just as Paul made the most of his last words to the Ephesus leaders, he concluded his letter to the Colossians with a similar intensity. There were some important final thoughts he wanted to express before he said good-bye and personally signed his letter. He desired they would be diligent in prayer, wait on the Lord's direction, walk in wisdom, speak carefully, and abound in grace. His passionate pleas for them to follow hard after the Lord are palpable.

As you finish up this last lesson from the book of Colossians, consider how God has used Paul to instruct countless people on how to minister in the name of Christ, including yourself through this study. Consider how you have been challenged, encouraged, and strengthened to be a woman who God can minister through to the people He places around you. Because you have been "rooted and built up in Him and established in the faith, as you have been taught" (Col. 2:7), you are ready to be a witness and example in His name. May the Lord bless you as you go forth!

RECEIVING GOD'S WORD

Open in Prayer

Read Colossians 4:2–18

EXPERIENCING GOD'S WORD

EXPERIENCE 1: DOING THE WORK OF THE LORD

Colossians 4:2–6

Pray

1. You may recall in the beginning of the book of Colossians Paul started his letter by sharing how he prayed for the believers in Colosse (Colossians 1:9-12). As we come to the close of the book, he also ends with the topic of prayer, asking the church in Colosse to pray for him and those serving with him. Read Colossians 4:2. Paul gives three characteristics for our prayer life. Write them below and answer the questions from the supporting verses.

   a. Characteristic 1: _____
       Read Acts 12:1–10. Describe how this characteristic of prayer impacted Peter.

       How would this have encouraged both Peter and those praying?

   b. Characteristic 2: _____
       Read Nehemiah 4:1–23. How did Nehemiah and his co-laborers apply this prayer characteristic?

How might this have increased their faith and alleviated any fear they had?

   c.   Characteristic 3: _____
       Read Daniel 2:1–23. How did Daniel exhibit this prayer characteristic?

How does this characteristic demonstrate both humility toward God and faith in Him?

DEEPER EXPERIENCE

"There is no power in dull, listless praying. If there is no fire on the altar, the incense will not rise to God (Psalm 141:2). Real praying demands spiritual energy and alertness, and this can come only from the Holy Spirit of God." (Warren Wiersbe, Be Complete, p.152)

2. Read Colossians 4:3. How does Paul apply these prayer characteristics to himself as he is address-ing the believers in Colosse? How is this a model for all of us in ministry?

DEEPER EXPERIENCE

"You as a church member, can assist your pastor in the preaching of the Word by praying for him. Never say to your pastor, 'Well, the least I can do is pray for you.' The most you can do is to pray! Pray for your pastor as he prepares the Word, studies, and meditates. Pray that the Holy Spirit will give deeper insights into the truth of the Word. Pray too that your pastor will practice the Word that he preaches so that it will be real in his own life. As he preaches the message, pray that the Spirit will give him freedom of utterance, and that the Word will reach into hearts and minds in a powerful way. (It wouldn't hurt to pray for other church leaders too.)" (Warren Wiersbe, Be Complete, p.155)

Wait

1. Read Colossians 4:3. What is Paul waiting for?

2. As God gives opportunities to Paul to share the gospel, Paul is concerned about two main things in Colossians 4:3–4. What are they?

    a. Read Ephesians 3:1–9. How is the mystery of Christ described?

3. How is Paul an example to those who serve the Lord while experiencing opposition?

Walk

1. Read Colossians 4:5 and then answer the following questions:

    a. What does Paul mean when he says to "walk in wisdom?"

    b. Read Proverbs 1:1–7. Describe a wise person according to these verses.

    c. Paul emphasizes a believer's wise walk in Ephesians 5:8–16. What characterizes a believer's "walk in wisdom?"

    d. Who is Paul referring to when he says, "Those who are on the outside?" What are they outside of?

    e. Read 1 Timothy 3:7. How does this verse connect "walking in wisdom" to your testimony to those who are "outside?"

    f. How does walking in wisdom redeem the time?

Speak

1. Read Colossians 4:6. Paul addresses the way a person speaks. What does he say about our words?

2. Read the following verses and write what you learn about gracious language.

   Proverbs 16:24

   Ephesians 4:29

   Colossians 3:16

3. Read Mathew 5:13 and Mark 9:50. Think about salt as a mineral in our world and the qualities salt possesses. Describe what it inherently has the power to accomplish.

   a. In Matthew 5:13 and Mark 9:50, Jesus compares a believer with salt. In Colossians 4:6, Paul links salt with a believer's words. What is he suggesting?

4. Paul reminds us in Colossians 4:6 that the way we interact with others in conversation is impactful. Read 1 Peter 3:15–16. Why is gracious and salty speech so important?

EXPERIENCE 2: CO-LABORERS IN CHRIST

Colossians 4:7–15

1. Read Colossians 4:7–8 and answer the following questions:

   a. How does Paul describe Tychicus in Colossians 4:7?

   b. Because Tychicus will know the circumstances of the church at Colosse, what will he be able to do well? Why?

2. Read Colossians 4:9. How does Paul describe Onesimus? How will he assist Tychicus?

   a. The book of Philemon is a short, one-chapter book in the New Testament. The purpose of the book was to write to a slave owner named Philemon regarding his runaway slave named Onesimus who became a believer when he met Paul. Read Philemon verses 1–25. What is Paul asking his friend Philemon to do on behalf of Onesimus?

3. Read Colossians 4:10. Aristarchus is mentioned as a co-laborer with Paul. According to Acts 19–20, Aristarchus was with Paul during the riot at Ephesus and traveled with him to Macedonia. Aristarchus was also with Paul on his voyage to Rome when he was shipwrecked (Acts 27:2). What additional information do you learn about Aristarchus from Colossians 4:10?

   a. How is Aristrachus an example of a faithful co-laborer?

4. Mark, also known as John Mark (Acts 12:12), wrote the Gospel of Mark. Mark and Paul had an encounter in Acts. Read Acts 15:36–41 and note what you learn about this interaction.

   a. Read Colossians 4:10 and 2 Timothy 4:11. What can you conclude has occurred between Paul and John Mark?

   b. How does this example serve as an encouragement when disagreements occur in ministry?

5. In Colossians 4:11 another co-laborer is named. Scripture doesn't give us any further information on this man named Justus, but Paul ends this verse by commending all the men he has mentioned in verses 7–11. What complimentary things does he say about them?

   a. How do these men offer an example for all who serve the Lord together?

6. It has been suggested that Epaphras may have been the founder of the church at Colosse. Read Colossians 4:12–13. How does Epaphras serve the church in Colosse?

   a. What was Paul and Epaphras' desire for the believers in Colosse according to verse 12?

7. In Colossians 4:14 we learn that Luke and Demas are with Paul. Read 2 Timothy 4:10–11. What happened between Demas and Paul after Paul wrote this letter to the Colossians? What do you learn about Luke as well?

8. In Colossians 4:15 how do you see Paul's zeal for the gospel as well as his love for God's people, especially those who are co-laborers?

EXPERIENCE 3: JUST DO IT!

Colossians 4:16–18

Share

1. Read Colossians 4:16. Paul's ministry covered the span of about 30 years. From what you've learned about Paul, obstacles did not stop his mission to share the gospel. Imprisonment didn't even stop him. How did his imprisonment change the way he had to share the gospel?

   a. Read Colossians 2:1. This verse explains Paul's burden for Laodicea. Now read Colossian 4:13. It is believed that Laodicea, as well as Hierapolis, was a church plant from Colosse. How is Paul's burden for these people still evident from verse 16?

2. Read 1 Timothy 4:13. Later Paul would write words of encouragement to his fellow servant, Timothy. How does this encouragement overlap with the encouragement given in Colossians 4:16?

3. Colossians 4:17 mentions Archippus, whom you met in Philemon 1:2. It is believed that Archippus had a church in his house. Paul encourages Archippus. What does he tell him?

    a. What important truth about ministry is seen in this verse?

4. Read the following verses about fulfilling the ministries that God has entrusted to our care. What do you learn about your responsibility and God's equipping?

    1 Corinthians 1:26–31

    Philippians 1:6

    Hebrews 13:20–21

5. Paul often dictated his letters. Read Colossians 4:18. What does Paul do to authenticate this letter to the Colossians. Why would this be important, especially to a group of people who had never met him?

6. In Colossians 4:18 Paul asks his audience to remember his chains. Read Hebrews 13:3. How are we to remember those in chains?

7. Read Colossians 4:18 and 1 Peter 4:8. Paul finishes with the statement, "Grace be with you all." Why is exhibiting grace a perfect capstone to the book of Colossians?

ACTING ON GOD'S WORD

In Colossians 4:2–18 Paul gave us a model to follow for all who minister in the name of Jesus Christ. His model isn't just for the servant herself but also for those who are serving beside you for the gospel. It applies to anyone who is serving the Lord individually or collectively. It applies to specific areas of ministry, like the Delighting in the Lord ministry, as well as the ministry of the worldwide church collectively and the ministry that happens within the four walls of our homes that often goes unseen by others.

I know Brenda and I are so thankful for those who serve with us in the DITL ministry. As they fulfill their ministry, they allow us to fulfill ours. It is a beautiful picture to behold! We also know that as our hearts are united in Christ, we are united in the work of the ministry from writing, editing, publishing, teaching, facilitating small groups, ministering one-on-one to the women, recording the messages, and all the administration that takes place behind the scenes. There are many who are co-laborers in this ministry with us for which we are so grateful. Paul's example is one that Brenda and I seek to employ, and we pray you do too as God calls you to serve Him.

In the verses studied, we looked at Paul's model. Now let's take these same ministry principles and apply them to ourselves. I've given you the same headings that were in the Experiencing part of the lesson and listed them with questions on the next two pages.

Pray

Throughout Paul's letter to the Colossian church, he stressed the importance of prayer for himself, other believers, and his co-laborers in Christ. How does Paul's teaching and request for prayer challenge your prayer life?

Our church, Calvary Chapel Chester Springs, supports many missionaries around the world who need prayer. Either through our church or other churches, find out the names of three missionary families you can pray for regularly. Use Paul's pleas for himself in Colossians 4:2–5 as a model, if you'd like. Write the names of the missionaries below as well as a few facts about them. Will you commit to praying for them in earnest?

Wait

As Paul was in chains, he waited on the Lord to both release him from his situation and/or for opportunities to share the gospel despite his imprisonment. Are you waiting on the Lord to open a door of ministry? What can you be doing for the Lord as you wait on Him?

Walk

The way you conduct yourself says a lot about your inner spiritual life, especially to a person who does not know the Lord personally. How does Paul's life, both as a servant of God as well as a minister of the gospel, give you an example to follow? How did the lives of his co-laborers also give you an example to follow?

Speak

Paul stressed the importance of our language as servants of the Lord. Your words matter! Think about your last communication either by phone, email, or text. What would your words reveal to someone who may not know you if they saw this last communication? How were your words gracious? How were they seasoned?

If God-honoring language is an area of struggle for you, what have you learned from the book of Colossians that you can apply to this area of life?

<u>**Share**</u>
Paul ends with a final exhortation to the church at Colosse regarding Archippus. He tells the church to encourage Archippus in his calling and ministry. Anyone serving the Lord knows the sacrifice required, the obstacles that come, the loneliness that can occur as well as the steadfastness required. How can you encourage a brother or sister in the Lord who is actively serving the Lord? Ask God to show you how you can put this encouragement into action.

<u>**Overall Study Take-Aways**</u>
What were the take-away instructions, exhortations, and/or encouragements that you learned from your study in Colossians?

How have you seen the Lord do a transformative work in your heart through your study of Colossians?

DELIGHTING IN GOD'S WORD DEVOTIONAL

"...Take heed to the ministry which you have received in the Lord, that you may fulfill it."
Colossians 4:17

As a young girl growing up in upstate New York, long, snow packed winters were expected. The first snow would come around Thanksgiving and would last clear through March. Living on a hill in rural New York, our home was exposed to the frequent blankets of snow and blowing wind with each snowstorm. I (Stacy) loved the playground the snow offered us, but my mother had quite another relationship with the snow. It was her mission to minimize the snow's effect on our home so that we could come and go as needed without being snowed in.

Knowing this about the winters, she quickly abandoned her love for planting perennial gardens and turned to planting trees. Our household ran on a limited income, and there were no male hands to help do the planting. Therefore, my sisters and I were tasked with planting itty bitty evergreen trees in the hopes that one day they would become an expansive snow fence to shield our home from the snow and wind. Under my mother's step-by-step instructions, we used our shovels and planted the young trees.

The tiny evergreen saplings had a focused mission unbeknownst to them, and we did too. It was a family effort to tend to them so they would establish deep roots and grow into a strong protective evergreen wall. With each passing winter, we waited. Year by year, the trees slowly grew into the barrier my mom had envisioned at the time they were planted. Finally, their mission was accomplished, and we all celebrated the protection the trees would provide in the winters to come.

Each of us has a God-given and God-driven mission to fulfill. Some of us are called to be planters, some water and care for what was planted, and as we saw in Colossians 4 some are called to prayerfully intercede for the planters and caretakers. There are still others who are called to pick up a shovel and come alongside someone serving the Lord and His people. Whatever ministry God calls you to, whether it's to be like the protective wall of trees for someone serving or the one digging deep into the soil, do what God is asking of you; pray, seek God, wait for open doors, and then when He says, "Speak" or "Do," fulfill the ministry God has entrusted to your care.

<u>**Praise God**</u> for the opportunities He gives you to serve Him.
<u>**Delight**</u> in the many gifts and roles God gives to His people.
<u>**Rest**</u> in God's equipping and grace as you fulfill your ministry in His name.

Close in Prayer

Teaching Title _____

_____

_____

_____

_____

_____

_____

_____

_____

_____

_____

_____

_____

_____

_____

_____

_____

_____

_____

_____

_____

_____

_____

Teaching Videos Available for free at www.delightinginthelord.com

AMG Publishers. *Hebrew-Greek Key Word Study Bible: Key Insights into God's Word*. AMG Publishers International, 2015.

Barton, Bruce B., and Philip Wesley Comfort. *Philippians, Colossians, Philemon*. Tyndale House Publishers, 1995.

Barker, Kenneth. *Expositor's Bible Commentary Abridged Edition*, 2004.

Phillips, John. *Exploring Colossians & Philemon: An Expository Commentary*. Kregel Publications, 2002.

Walvoord, John F., and Roy B. Zuck. *The Bible Knowledge Commentary: New Testament*. David C. Cook, 1983.

Wiersbe, Warren W. *Be Complete: Become the Whole Person God Intends You to Be*. David C. Cook, 2008.

www.biblegateway.com

www.blueletterbible.org

www.dictionary.com/browse/let?s=t

www.enterthebible.org/resourcelink.aspx?rid=1111

www.merriam-webster.com/dictionary/asceticism

www.merriam-webster.com/dictionary/gnosticism

www.merriam-webster.com/dictionary/legalism

www.nsf.gov/discoveries/disc_images.jsp?cntn_id=114979

www.unsplash.com/photos/lYfm-wA3yWU

Delighting in the King of Kings: Matthew Volume 1: Chapters 1–9 (Amazon) 9 Weeks

Delighting in the King of Kings: Matthew Volume 2: Chapters 10–20 (Amazon) 11 Weeks

Delighting in the King of Kings: Matthew Volume 3: Chapters 21–28 (Amazon) 8 Weeks

28 Week Study Total

Study the life of the King of Kings, Jesus Christ, from His birth to His ascension from the perspective of the gospel writer Matthew. This series is written as a three-volume set but can be studied individually.

Delighting in God's Wisdom: Proverbs (Amazon)
13 Week Study
Gain wisdom from the book of Proverbs while learning from examples of women in the Bible. King Solomon is the primary writer of this book and sets forth insights on how to solve many of life's challenges.

Delighting in a Life of Triumph: A Study on the Life of Joseph from Genesis 37–50 (Amazon)
9 Week Study
Examine what triumphant living can look like, even when faced with challenging family relationships, being wrongly accused, and forgotten by those who should have loved you. The life of Joseph is a powerful testimony about how to live victoriously amidst life's difficult circumstances.

Delighting in a Life Lived for God: A Study on the Book of 1 Peter (Amazon)
10 Week Study
Study the encouragement given by the disciple Peter on how to live a perfected, established, strengthened, and settled life in the Lord while in the midst of difficulty, trials, and persecution.

Delighting in Being a Woman of God: Esther
8 Week Study
See how God impacted the entire Jewish nation through the life of one God-ordained woman named Esther. This study reminds us that God can use anyone who is obedient to His call to impact their generation.

Delighting in the Holy Spirit: Acts
26 Week Study
Learn about the early church and how it was established in the powerful book of Acts. Miracles, wonders, and life-altering events are documented in Acts as the Holy Spirit was poured out on the people of God, forever changing lives.

Delighting in God's Heart:
A Study on the Life of David through 1 & 2 Samuel and the Psalms
24 Weeks
David remains hailed as one of Israel's greatest kings. Meet this remarkable man as he rises up out of the shepherd field to eventually sit upon the throne to rule his nation. Many of David's joys and sorrows are recorded in the Psalms which accompany this study to give us a more complete picture of David, a man after God's own heart.

Delighting in Our Redeemer: Ruth
4 Week Study
Glean from the life of Ruth how to emulate love, honor, and loyalty. Her story is a reflection of God's love and redemption toward His beloved.

Delighting in God's Will and His Provision: Jonah & Nahum
7 Week Study
Two prophets give the same message, "Repent!" Jonah's message was received, and God's grace was demonstrated toward the people of Nineveh. About 100 years later Nahum arrived with the same plea because wickedness had returned to the region of Assyria (Ninevah being its capital), and this time judgment would come to the unrepentant city. When studied together, Jonah and Nahum portray the accurate picture of how God is both loving and just.

Delighting in Being a Child of God: 1, 2 & 3 John
8 Week Study
The last living apostle, John, gives his final instructions to the early believers and describes God's love for His children.

Delighting in God, His Righteousness, and Perfect Plan: Romans
17 Week Study
Because Paul desired for the Christians in Rome to understand God's plan of salvation through Jesus Christ, Paul wrote to them prior to his arrival. This book sets forth man's fallen condition, the forgiveness available through Jesus Christ, and the life of freedom that is available to everyone.

For additional information about the ministry, please go to:

www.delightinginthelord.com
www.cc-chestersprings.com/DITL
(Download for free any study and view videos from the teachings)

For weekly encouragement, follow Delighting in the Lord on Facebook

Made in the USA
Monee, IL
05 November 2024